Paul Richards was born in Finchley, North London in 1933. During World War Two he was evacuated to Cookham on Thames. The author passed exams that enabled him to attend Windsor County Boys School. Paul returned to Cricklewood in London after the war with his parents. He then attended Holloway Grammar School and attained matriculation.

The author next became an apprentice motor mechanic in Cumberland Garage, Marble Arch. He served as craftsman in R.E.M.E. Malaysia during the emergency. Paul then became the managing director of Luton hat manufacturing company, Richards & Thirkell (Luton) Ltd. for more than thirty years, until his retirement.

## Dedication

With love and best wishes to my three grandsons:

JAMES          CHRISTIAN          JACK

Paul Richards

# BETTER A FRIEND THAN A FOE!

## LIFE WITH THE GURKHAS

AUSTIN MACAULEY

6 835 041 000

A CIP catalogue record for this title is available from the British Library.

ISBN 978 178455 115 5

www.austinmacauley.com

First Published (2014)
Austin Macauley Publishers Ltd.
25 Canada Square
Canary Wharf
London
E14 5LB

Printed and bound in Great Britain

The year 1951 should have been a joyful and continuing recovery year, from the hard and difficult years of the Second World War and the then Labour government was doing its best to promote that "feel good" element into the nation by putting on a good show to its own people, and to the world, in the form of the Festival of Britain. This was a national exhibition throughout the UK in the summer of 1951.

The centrepiece was the Royal Festival Hall in London, situated on the South Bank. Battersea Pleasure Gardens was also associated with the Labour government, under the leadership of Clement Attlee. Interest rates were cut to just 2% by the Bank of England, the lowest for fifty seven years. On the tenth of January, the United Nations Head Quarters opened in Manhattan New York, and the British Post Office marked the Festival of Britain with a festival icon, on the four penny issue stamp.

However, with all the good news at home, things were far from satisfactory in other parts of the world, particularly, the Far East. The Korean War had commenced, and fierce fighting right along the whole front was extremely serious. On the first of January, 1951, there was a massive assault by the Chinese and Koreans on the South Korean lines, and despite the strong lines of UN troops and the heavy bombarding of North Korea by the Americans, it was the sheer numbers of the Chinese and North Koreans that attacked, wave after wave, which were gaining ground, despite the forward positioned machine gunners of the UN killing many thousands of the enemy.

Continuing into April 1951, the twenty second to the twenty first, saw the battle of the Imjin River. The $29^{th}$.Infantary Brigade of the British army, serving with the UN, put up a very brave resistance to the Chinese advance, but ultimately was unsuccessful, and some 141 United Nations troops were killed. The stand of the $1^{st}$ Battalion of the Gloucestershire regiment at Hill 235 became part of modern military history ... the Glorious Glosters!

**Roll call of the Gloucester survivors of the Battle of the Imjin River, Korea 1951**

Also going on in the Far East was the Malaysian Emergency, a campaign that had commenced in 1948 just three years after the Second World War. Once again the communist insurgent forces started a guerrilla war, this time to end British rule in Malaya. They were infiltrating over the northern border of Malaya, from Thailand. The Malayan Communist Party, and guerrilla organisation, The Malayan Peoples Anti-Japanese Army, generally known as, M.P.A.J.A. had conceived a plan of political agitation and terrorism in Malaya. It was a pattern of armed struggle throughout Asia. Murder and intimidation of Malaya, Indian, and Chinese, and particularly the rubber plantations, which were usually owned by British companies, and more often or not managed by Europeans, particularly the English.

At this point, it may be prudent to give a little more information about the MPAJA. Resistance of the Japanese occupation was very much the work of this organisation, which was assisted at that time by the British with many types of weapons and ammunitions hidden in the jungle by them, and to be used by them, and in addition certain airdrops of arms and ammunition were made. Some 5,000 of these men and women were experts in the jungle terrain, and very much up to giving the Japanese occupation forces a very difficult time. They had learned how to survive on the fruits of the jungle, in addition to the rice and things that were supplied to them by villagers that were willing to risk their lives. Now it was said that the British government had promised these fighting men and women that when the Japanese were beaten, and the war against them won, the British government of the day would reward the fighters with money, according to the weapons they surrendered, with a fixed monetary reward according to the weapon. Now here comes the contentious issue, and to this day, nobody has said if it is the truth, or a lie. The rumour was that when the members of the MPAJA started to hand in their weapons the British government only gave them about half the amount promised. In anger, they turned again the British government, and sided with the MCP (Malayan Communist Party), led by Chin Peng, who would lead them to fight the British for twelve years, from 1948 to 1960. To my knowledge, this story has no real proof, but on the other hand, there does not appear to be any denial on record, from the British government, so one wonders if it was just a story made up by certain people, who disliked the British so very much!

For me 1951 was just another year, living at home in Cricklewood, North West London, with my parents. I was a trainee motor mechanic, at the Cumberland Garage, Marble Arch, at that time part of the Joe Lyons group of companies. Most days of the year, when the weather was good, I could cycle the few miles from Cricklewood, along the Edgware Road, to my place of work.

Back in the UK at that time, National Service was mandatory for all young men when they reached the age of 18 years. There were a few exceptions to the rule, dependant on what work you were training for; if you were at university, a conscientious objector, and a few other reasons, then you could have your National Service deferred.

For me, aged 18 years on the 30th of January, 1951, it was my turn, the thing to do ... to serve one's country! There was a choice, if one could use such a word, but the powers that be would make the final decision of army, navy or air force. It was always difficult for young men to get into the navy, as the training period was much longer than for the other two services.

Not long after my birthday, I was given written notice to attend a military medical centre in Acton, West London. There were hundreds of us. We were instructed to remove all clothing, and then form a line, and, one by one, we were ushered into a large room, where there were several doctors, and medical attendants, with clip boards, note pads, and the like. Many questions were asked about your health, whilst your chest and back were sounded by stethoscope; bodies were tapped, hair, eyes, tongues were inspected, and the usual, please "cough" treatment was carried out; until, finally, we were dismissed, to dress once again.

There was then a few weeks of waiting, and I was able to return to my home and place of work. Then through the letterbox one day, came that special letter, O.H.M.S., and a rail ticket which would take me to Blandford, in Dorset, to the Number 1 Training Battalion R.E.M.E. It seemed to me that the army had been most sensible in sending me to the regiment of Royal Electrical & Mechanical Engineers, which would be completely in line with my apprenticeship at the Cumberland Garage. One had heard rumours in the past of a skilled mechanic in civvy street being sent into the army as a cook; or of a brick layer in civvy street ending up in the army as a medical orderly. It happened!

Several of us 18 year olds were on the train that day; mostly happy lads to whom the inevitable had happened, and the sensible thing to do was to make the best of it. Then there were a couple that were not very happy, and were certainly not going to enjoy the next few weeks.

On arriving at Blandford station, there was a military vehicle waiting our arrival to take us to the camp. The camp was somewhat isolated, and somewhat desolate, in the middle of what, we were later told, was a motor cycle race course. I do not remember which came first, the kitting out, with all the uniform and equipment we would ever need, or the hair cut. At that period of the 1950s a hair style had to include the quiff, hair standing up at the front of the head, and neatly combed backwards. That soon disappeared with a few deft strokes of the barbers trimmer, which he appeared to like, much more that a comb and scissors. It was however not catastrophic, but certainly short back and sides was the order of the day. The speed with which he performed each and every hair cut was amazing, so we all guessed he was on piece work.

We were duly marched to our billet, one of many on the camp. A wooden structure, with windows either side, and housing around twenty beds, ten either side, with a small wardrobe by each bed. There was a stove fire in the centre of the building, with a long pipe, disappearing out through the roof. This was to be home for the next four or five weeks, maybe a little longer. The whole room was not that warm, certainly when days were cold and damp. Everyone had been given his army number, which, strangely enough, you never forgot, and mine was 22476768. It comes to mind so easily and yet, what I had for breakfast yesterday, I have quite possibly forgotten!

Within a short time of being in our billet, there was the sound of marching feet, and into the billet marched two soldiers, one with two stripes on his sleeve, and the other with three stripes on his sleeve. They introduced themselves, the tallest, about 6ft 2 inches with the two stripes, was Corporal Butcher. A fine, healthy looking individual and the second was Sergeant Marsh, shorter, and thicker set. He spoke with a distinctively Irish brogue. It was Marsh who explained that it was their duty, to turn us unruly teenagers, into men ... into soldiers of the British army within a very limited time. He also went on to tell us, perhaps just for good measure, that he had been doing this particular job for a number of years, and that he had never failed to carry out the transformation, from youth to men, despite the many difficulties he had had, from time to time, but assured us that whatever we thought, we could rest assured that whatever it took to do it, it would be done!

Kitting out was something for which you had to pay particular attention, as the quartermaster was a professional of the highest order, shouting out each item, as he placed them before you on the counter. Just by observation he could calculate the size of jacket, trousers, shirt, and most other things you needed, and every now and then make a cursory check with his inch tape. Articles were shouted out precisely in typical military jargon ... Beret, wool, navy blue! You had to be extremely alert as you were fully responsible for each and every item, down to the *REME metal beret badge, and you had to sign the infantry and if you were short of an item at a later inspection, you had to pay for a replacement, lost damaged or otherwise.

I then learned that I had been allocated to "B" company, number 5 platoon, which was the baby of Sergeant Marsh and Corporal Butch. Neither of them had actually mentioned that, at the time of their introduction, but it was good to know. Further information which we gradually learned was that there would be great competition from the other platoons, as their respective sergeants and corporals, would all be looking to have the best platoon at the end of the training, at the passing out parade. We looked forward to a tough time ahead!

*Looking at a REME insignia, the slang interpretation for newcomers was:

**Work like a horse, move like grease lightning and don't drop a bollock, but lower it gently to the ground on a chain.**

It was obvious from the start that Sergeant Marsh was not to be messed with, and certainly you would be sensible to obey his every instruction and command or bear the consequences. Marsh often carried a stick under his armpit. It was not a pace stick or a swagger stick, but something which helped his ego in believing that he was a sergeant major, and not just a sergeant.

Day started at 6.00 a.m. with much bawling and shouting by our two NCOs, ensuring that we were well awake and on our way to the showers. It was not the best time of the year to be having an early morning shower, as the water was invariably cold ... and very cold! After dressing rapidly, it was off to the cookhouse for breakfast. Now in fairness to the army, you do get a good cooked breakfast. You filled your own metal mug with tea from a large tea urn, and there were several of them. Standing in line, and holding out your metal plate, you would proceed along a line of army cooks, members of the Army Catering Corps. The first would possibly drop a fried egg onto your plate, the second cook, a sausage, then the bacon, and finally, the inevitable baked beans. It was then up to you to wash and dry your utensils, plate, mug, which you carried back to your billet.

I soon became friendly with two other conscripts, one either side of my bed. It so happened that the first letter of their surname was very close to mine, and at that time, did not realise that because of this, we would possibly be spending quite some time together. Merlin Rhodes was one lad, and he came from Hyde, near Manchester, the other Gerry Preston, and he was from the Birmingham area. Both Gerry and Merlin had been training in civvy street to become motor mechanics, the same as me.

Daily tasks were often quite tough, as everything had to be done at the double, and your change over periods demanded changes in clothing, from time to time. As an example you may be in shorts and PT (physical training) vest, for an hour's session of exercise in the gym, this possibly involved work on the climbing ropes, a session of over the "horse" up the wall bars, and many other general exercises, and after all that, possibly a change into fatigue uniform, for an hour or more marching on the square outside. There may well be a whole session of marching, with rifles, and rifle drill. By this time, it would possibly be lunch time, and you would go through the same procedures as breakfast. There may be a beef stew, with mashed potatoes, peas and another vegetable, plus a sweet, possibly a sponge pudding with custard, so the food was quite substantial, and nourishing.

Now from time to time, the duty officer would do his rounds of the tables, and ask if there were any complaints. Basically, there was little to complain about, but if for instance you had got a piece of meat that was as tough as an old leather boot or a hair in your custard, it would be prudent of you not to complain, as no one ever knew what the outcome may be. It was always suggested, that you may well end up in the cookhouse washing dishes, and greasy pans the whole of the evening, and I feel sure it did happen, but I also feel sure that if some foreign body had been found in your food, and you were able to show the duty officer, and prove your case, it may well be the cooks would be in trouble. Still could be dangerous for you however, because if the cook found out that it was you that had complained you may well have a problem in the form of an "accident" when he was dishing out food onto your plate!

Your fitness level was increasing all the time, as whatever you ate was quickly burned off with the exercise, and this continued day after day. Precision marching, counter marching, moving in various directions and formations at various commands. Yes, Butcher and Marsh kept you at it mornings and afternoons. Field craft was interesting. Learning how to never get lost, no matter where you were; learning to crawl nearer and nearer to an object of position, such as the enemy, without being spotted. Yes, there certainly was a lot to learn. Bayonet drill. How to fit the bayonet promptly to your rifle and how to use it by thrusting it into a type of sacking, sandbags hanging from special frames, imitating and substituting for real bodies. Then we had the wall with two teams. The wall was high, and needed one lot of lads, bent over, against the wall, enabling others to leap onto their backs giving them height enough to get over the wall, and then those on top of the wall pulling the others up, then all of them dropping over the other side. Crossing muddy, deep water on a single rope beneath you, and one above, to steady you - not that easy!

Logical team tests, pretending to get heavy equipment over a stream, or river; an assault course, crawling under netting, through filthy water, and tunnels; everything was a great learning curve, and both Marsh and Butcher appeared intent on our platoon being the best. We were continually reminded that we were in serious competition with other platoons, run by equally demanding NCOs. We were not even an infantry platoon or brigade ... so why are we doing all this?

At the end of each day, the physical aspect of the training made most of us quite tired, but each evening we had various tasks to do, such as the ironing of our uniforms, shirts etc. Our boots had to be polished until you could see your face in the shiny toe part. This meant real spit and polish. A little spittle on the boot, then the black polish, alternately; then the Blanco, which had to be applied to your webbing belt, gaiters etc. Brass buckles and buttons to be polished, with "Brasso". At any time you could have an inspection, and this meant that you had to wear the lot. If a button was left undone, that was punishable. Dirty boots on the UNDERSIDE merited a punishment. Perfect creases in your trousers, and there could be no excuse for anything that was not perfect.

There were however, a few tricks which you could learn. If you scorched your uniform when ironing you could rub the scorch mark with a silver coin and make it disappear. Rub some wet soap inside your trouser seam, and then iron; that would make the seam sharp, and stay there for a long time. Little lead weights on a thin string band, just wider than your gaiters, and arrange the string of weights, just inside your trousers, overhanging the top of your gaiters, and looks very smart ... but do not get caught, it is illegal! ... And then your bedding. You had been taught that your pillow, your blankets and all bedding had to be made up at the head of the bed, or sometimes the end of the bed, folded to perfection in a special set way.

On inspection,and that was more or less daily, regardless of whether you were present or not, if you failed a bed inspection in any way, with any aspect of imperfection your bed, with all the bedding, was turned over, onto the floor. A punishment would usually follow. Punishments could vary, and could include marching around the parade square for a whole hour, possibly even with a weighty pack on your back, or it could mean cleaning your NCO's boots, blanco-ing their webbing, or maybe something else. One must appreciate that to obey every command, without question, to carry out bedding routines, ironing of uniforms etc., is all part of the British Army's' way of instilling total obedience from all its military. To put every soldier in a "no win" situation at all times. This is perhaps one of the main reasons why the British army has always been so successful wherever it has gone in the world, and in whichever battles it has fought. The men act on any command, without question, and this in itself has saved so many lives.

Back in the 1950s, and particularly for National Service, no one had ever heard of a thing called abuse. Human Rights or anything else had never been heard of, so that you were called all the names under the sun, your parentage, and your birth were often under fire, and as for swearing, I really do believe that Sergeant Marsh would have ended up a deaf mute, had he not been able to swear in his broad Irish brogue.

One thing you had to watch very carefully with Marsh, was, if you were on parade with your rifle, and you were not holding the rifle totally correctly, he would shout ... "Throw your f*****g rifle to me, you f*****g idiot," and you would throw it to him, but in a flash, he would possibly throw it back to you, and if you were not alert, you could end up with a broken nose, and no teeth! No, there was no Human Rights Act, no "mamby pamby" world, as it is today, so toughen up, and don't complain.

Before going onto the firing range, it was important that you had a thorough knowledge of certain weapons, the three main weapons a soldier carried, would be the .303 rifle. Then there was the Sten gun, an inaccurate little automatic gun, looking a bit like a piece of lead piping, and the Bren gun, which was a pretty powerful automatic gun in its day. On the firing range, we used the .303. It was heavy, but pretty accurate; the Bren gun was accurate, and spewed out its spent bullets at quite a rate. The Sten gun we never used on the range, because I think that it was so inaccurate, that for novices like us, it could have been dangerous.

In order to know everything about these weapons, we had very thorough tuition on each of them, by breaking them down into their component parts and then re-assembling them, time and time again, until we could do it quickly and efficiently. We were also shown how to deal with a Bren gun when it jammed, which again was most important if it happened in actual battle. Cleaning, and "Pulling through" the barrel of each gun was a very important routine also. This expression meant, pulling a soft piece of cloth, through the whole length of the rifle barrel.

**Lightweight Bren Gun**

Once you are in the military, you are firstly a soldier of the British Army, and there is little doubt that this is why the British Army has always remained the best trained in the world, turning out the very best of military personnel for hundreds of years. Alter the many weeks of continuous training, the rag-tag assortment of lads, from all sorts of backgrounds, had become a smart, disciplined unit of professional soldiers.

The end result of all those weeks of hard training was the passing out parade; such an important day, for the NCOs that had been training you for the day when their skills and dedication would be pitted against others. An important day for each and every one of the platoons, to prove that one of them was better than the others, in drill and turnout.

The morning of the parade, everyone was up early, showered, had breakfast, and was back in the billet polishing boots for the final time, making sure that webbing was perfect, and that shirt, ties and uniform were pressed and looking like perfection. I was in the process of pressing my jacket, and then trousers, when around came Sergeant Marsh, and Corporal Butcher. They had already spoken with several of the lads on certain points which they had noticed were not to their high standard, and when they got to me, Marsh told me, in no uncertain terms that my trouser creases were not exactly correct, and I needed them to be done again, otherwise it could let down the whole platoon.

This I did immediately, making sure that the creases were exact from top to bottom, and no sign of a scorch mark!

We were now out on the parade ground, had now formed into perfect lines, upon which you could have run a measuring tape, and not found the slightest error. The inspection was a very tense period, as the inspecting officer, a colonel, as far as I recall, slowly but surely walked along each line, closely followed by another very senior officer, Sergeant Marsh, with a clip board, and Butcher following. Every now and then, the inspecting officer would stop, and speak to a soldier, and Marsh would make note. Because you are looking ahead, you cannot actually see them approaching, but you can feel them coming, and eventually, without almost a blink of my eyes, he was standing directly in front of me. He asked my name, he asked when I joined the army and then he said ... "Very smart turnout" ... and moved on. At that particular moment, Marsh and Butcher looked like a couple of cats, with two tails. Both had large smiles on their faces, and were without any doubt, more than pleased with the officer's comment. For me I was delighted, as it was only that morning that Marsh had chastised me, in no uncertain terms, because of the creases in my trousers, so I really felt, that it was one up to me! The final march past then took place, with the senior officer taking the salute. We were then permitted to "Fall out" and returned to our billet.

**The March Past on Passing Out Parade at Blandford**

We were all quite excited, and had reckoned that we had done well, but naturally did not know the final result, and who would be the winning platoon. It was not long, before both Marsh and Butcher appeared, to inform us that we had been elected as the winning platoon, and Marsh even congratulated me on the smart run out, as declared by the inspecting officer. Both NCOs were obviously overjoyed with that result, and informed us that if we liked to be at a certain local pub that evening they would be buying the drinks.

That evening most of us did go to the pub, and drinks were flowing, everyone was jovial, and Marsh and Butcher, were not the same people they had been over the past weeks. In fact they were likeable, and really no different to all of us lads.

At that point, it made me realise that these two NCOS, whose life was the army, do a very tough and important job for the military. They are really decent men, and not the bastards that you think they are during your training weeks. It is a task that today would be very difficult to match, as there are so many restrictions on what you can say, and do to others in such a limited time scale, they are a credit to themselves and the

British Army. They were far from the sadistic creatures that many outsiders think.

Now we were all in for a 72 hour leave, to return home to family and friends. We were notified that our time at Blandford was now completed, and that for myself, Gerry and Merlin, we would be posted to a camp near Taunton in Somerset ... Norton Manor, another REME training camp for mechanical and electrical training, mainly with civilian instructors. So this was something to look forward to. Back home in Cricklewood, my parents, and sister were naturally pleased to see me once again.

I arrived with all my worldly possessions, in my kit bag. Dad appeared to be quite proud that his son was now a soldier and celebrated by taking me to his favourite pub and having a few drinks, and some time together. The short break passed quickly, and once again I was on my way by train, to Norton Manor Camp, Taunton, travelling on my military train ticket.

At Taunton railway station there was an army vehicle waiting to pick me and any others up, and take us the few miles from the town of Taunton to Norton Manor. Once at the camp I met up with Gerry and Merlin, and a few others, who had arrived on earlier trains, and we were all attending the same vehicle mechanics course.

The billets were nice, roomier, more modern, and in fact the whole camp was very clean and tidy, and with a very relaxed atmosphere. Each day we would attend "school" where we had first class civilian instructors, who were obviously very skilled mechanics themselves, but most importantly of all, they were teachers, that were able to pass on their knowledge to us. A certain amount of our work was written work, theory etc., with many demonstrations, and hands on work in the workshops. Many questions you were asked were ones that would possibly never happen in civvy street, and sometimes appeared to be trick questions, but they were not. They were questions that needed to be thought about carefully before coming to any conclusion and one in particular I remember, which I, and others did not work out logically. The question posed was, "If you were called out to a large vehicle that had broken down in very hilly countryside, and that lorry towed your vehicle back to the workshop, what was his problem?" Initially it appears to be a tricky question, but after careful thought and consideration, the logical answer must be, that he had total brake failure! Although in civilian life at the Cumberland Garage I had a good mechanic with whom I worked daily, and who was teaching me everything which I needed to know, and was comprehensive, in that we dealt with all type of cars, such as the Jowett Javelin, the AC, the Riley, Austins, Fords, Chevrolet, Citroen, Buick, and many, many, more. I was actually learning more at Norton Manor, and particularly about diesel engines, which were very few and far between in cars in those days.

I was very much enjoying my time at Norton Manor, and the life in civvy street now appeared to be a million miles away. Even life at home was a distant thing of the past and I really did not miss family, but then that is possibly a normal thing for a young man of eighteen years of age. Most evenings we had time off, and some of us would venture into Taunton, and visit a pub or two. There certainly were amusing incidents involving local pubs and the local brew, for that was the "scrumpy" local Somerset cider, pretty raw, and often with little bits floating amongst the liquid, which one had always expected to be clear, when you had cider back home. Looking around the pub at the locals, they were all drinking half pints, and some of the lads thought that the locals were obviously not proper drinkers, as you would find back home, so pints were ordered by almost every one of the lads, who then commenced to quench their thirst, by downing almost half a pint in one go. Big mistake! Talking to some of the locals we soon realised that they had a very good reason for supping and sticking to their half pints at a time. Mind you, during the evening they would possibly down two pints or so ... but very slowly. Scrumpy is in fact a very potent cider, and because of its roughness, can make you very sick if drunk too quickly, and that was the case for several lads, as soon as they got out of the pub. For myself, I had been a little more sensible, and taken it easy, and had even left a half of my pint. From now on however, and having learned our lessons, only half pints were ordered, on other outings. During my time at Norton Manor, I did have to do two guard duties, as did most of us. This meant being in the guard room at the entrance to the camp, and making sure that you checked everyone coming in to the camp and departing.

The course lasted about four months, and at the end of the course there were final tests, which if passed, made you a Craftsman, in other words, a qualified vehicle mechanic. The day of the final test came, and everyone was swatting up on what the final questions could be. There was a large building which housed six engines down one side, and six down the other side These engines were mounted on steel frames, and the exhaust pipes from each engine, passed to the outside of the building. We were instructed to stand by a designated engine, and were then informed, than on each engine, there were five or six faults. Not every engine had the same faults however. We were then told that we had a given period of time, in which to sort out the faults and get the engines started. We were also informed that if one spotted an obvious fault, such as a wire hanging loose, or similar, we were not to go straight to it, but to follow the fault finding sequence, which we had been taught, and that there were four men, with clipboards, walking up and down from engine to engine watching our every move. These were the examiners.

One did feel that there was pressure there, but if we had absorbed all the information which we had been taught, things should go smoothly, but exam times can often be a little tense. After about three quarters of an hour, an engine was started, and soon after that, another started. Now with these engines running, it did put on the pressure, but not panic. You did realise that you needed to speed up a little and after hearing a third engine fire, I was ready to start my engine. It was quite a relief when my engine fired, and ticked over at a gentle pace, having found all the faults on it. An examiner came to me and said, "Well done, lad."

Leaving Norton Manor was a little sad, as it had been most enjoyable, compared to the time spent at Blandford.

We now had a 72 hour leave, or it may have been longer, I cannot remember for sure, but this gave us the opportunity to get home to see family and friends once again. For those lads that lived in Scotland, that was tough on them.

Our next posting was to Aborfield, in Berkshire. This was a REME draft depot, which meant for sure, that we were all going to be sent abroad. There were many places in the world that we could be sent because the British Army was well spread. There was Hong Kong, which was a quiet posting, with no trouble. There was Germany, another "cushy" posting, and many more around the world. Then there was Aden, in the Yemen, in which there was possibly trouble brewing, mainly tribal. There was Egypt, the Suez Canal region, where there had been unrest, and there already a good number of troops there. Then there was the Korean war, between the north and the south, with the south being supported by UK troops, and the north Koreans supported by the Chinese. The Malayan Emergency was causing a lot of problems, and was getting worse, so there were a lot of possibilities for us. The one thing we did know for sure was that we would be sent to one of these locations.

With the Korean War still raging, and the Malaysian Emergency still continuing, it was pretty obvious that both theatres of war would need to replace men who had done their terms there. Korea would obviously have the most casualties, and would need the greater number of replacements, as this was a real war and could not be compared to the Malayan Emergency, where, although there was a combination of more than 150,000 armed troops, and police, the actual casualty rate was very much lower, if one can put that into context!

I had arrived at Arborfield, and once again met up with many lads that I had known from the past. Arborfield was a very large camp, with people moving in and out on a daily basis. Our bedding was something that nobody enjoyed, as one had to sleep on a palliasse. Now for those that have never slept at one, it is cotton, or sometimes nylon bag, shaped to the size of a bed, length and width wise, and is filled with straw. There are sharp bits of straw and things, which protrude through the material, and make rest or sleep, somewhat uncomfortable. Now add to that a blanket, which is rough in its texture anyway, and does not smell that sweet, as I am sure they were rarely washed; soldiers being issued with them on arrival, then handing them back a few days or weeks later, to be handed out to the next soldier. Head end or feet end, you could only judge by the smell. Sheets were unheard of. Just by chance, whilst I was at Arborfield I did come across an old school friend of mine from my days at Holloway Grammar School, in North London. He was being shipped out to Hong Kong within a few days` time

I did not realise that I would be in Arborfield for quite a few weeks, and this particular camp did seem to be in the middle of nowhere, so there was not a lot to do or places to go to outside of camp even if you wanted to. It does appear that the army almost always has camps far away from civilisation, but that is perhaps because the general public do not feel that an army camp right on their doorstep, is the appropriate thing.

Inside camp, there were morning parades and attendance checks, plus tasks that you were given like attending the officers' mess to be doing a bit of waiting. I was instructed to report one morning to the sergeant cook at the cookhouse, where food was prepared, cooked and served to senior officers. The kitchen was a standard type of military kitchen, with all the usual equipment, including a large double gas cooker. Above the cooker was a rack for clean plates, that had been washed, and dried, but they continued to get the benefit of heat from the gas jets on the cooker and it was upon these plates that the sergeant cook, Army Catering Corps, used to hang his socks to dry. There was always a large tea urn situated upon the cooker, and from its tap, one was supposed to fill the teapots, which could then be taken to each table, making the whole thing look a little bit more upmarket, with a milk jug, and decent tea cups, and spoons. This was a job I was to do for around a week or more, and on one particular day, I along with another "waiter," was having quite a problem in getting the tea, from the urn into the tea pot. Although the tap was in the "on" position, little tea was coming forth, so we called over the sergeant. He fiddled for some time, without success, and then realised that the top of the urn had been left open, and two pairs of his socks had dropped into the urn, and had possibly been simmering away for an hour or two! He hooked them out, and they all looked a good colour, because the dye from the tea had made them a little darker in colour than normal. Without further notice, we filled the tea pots, delivered the tea to tables, and not one complaint was made on its quality!

Quite a few weeks passed at the draft pool, and one was thankful that there was always the good old NAAFI to go to, and get a drink, and have a chat with some of the lads. We were informed that some of us would be going to Singapore, and that included me. At that particular time, perhaps through my ignorance, I thought of only Singapore, which was a posting anyway, and it did not dawn on me, that once in Singapore, just across the causeway, was Malaya, and a theatre of war! I was given formal notice of this posting, and given a 72 hour leave and told to report to London on a certain day, at a certain time, and that I would be catching a special troop train to Liverpool, where we would sail from, to get to Singapore.

That due date quickly arrived, and I said goodbye to my parents and sister, and had previously said goodbye to my grandparents, one pair who lived in Hampstead and the others in Cricklewood. For me, it was perhaps a mixture of sadness, and of happiness. Sadness, because I knew that I would be away for some time, and my grandparents were getting on in years and like most families at that time, grandparents were very much an integral part of anyone's family. The other was the excitement of the fact that I was going to such a faraway land, as in those days, people of my age had possibly never gone further abroad than the Isle of Wight. I had, however, as a lad at school, been on a school holiday to France, and to Italy, but that was all. Other holidays, I recall, were in such places as Bracklesham Bay, and the like ... not that exciting! The ship would take about six weeks to get to Singapore from the UK, so I was in for a long holiday, at the expense of the government, and army.

Arriving in London to catch the troop train was an experience on its own. Troops everywhere, of all different regiments, complete with kitbags, stating name and number, two thousand of them, although it seemed more. Two hundred females, of the Queen Alexandra's Royal Army Nursing Corps, and all on the way to Liverpool.

As the train pulled out of the station, there was much hand waving from the train windows, and farewells. The train moved slowly, as we often had to stop, to allow other trains to pass, and it took all day long to get to Chester, where we were able to spend the night at the HQ of the Cheshire Regiment's barracks. The following morning after breakfast we were on our way again, and arrived at the docks in Liverpool, where waiting alongside was our troopship, the Empress of Australia. A large, three funnel ship, not of particularly modern design, and appearance, but that was because it had a very long and interesting history. It had been built at the Vulcan Shipyard in Stettin (which is now Szczecin-Poland) in 1913. It was an important German ship at the time of its construction, and was named Admiral Von Tirpitz, and later the name altered to, Tirpitz in 1914.

In 1929 it was used as a cruise ship, and was painted white throughout. At the end of 1946 she had been acquired by the British, and was sent to Belfast, and totally refitted, as a full time troop ship, at Harland & Wolff.

Her last trip would be the one we were going on, and she eventually returned from this trip on the 29th of April 1952, to Liverpool.

**The Empress of Australia**

The speed of the ship was 19.5 knots and the gross tonnage, 21,800, and she was meant to carry some 1,975 passengers. We boarded the ship on the 3$^{rd}$ of December, 1951. This took the whole day, as the troops had to be dispersed to the various areas of the ship, keeping in mind that there were families of certain senior officers, and also the contingent of Queen Alexandra's nurses. These were completely separated from the male soldiers, and the women's area was totally, out of bounds.

The accommodation was for us a large area, full of dining tables and benches, and after collecting our food from the galley, we were able to think about eating, and then perhaps bedding down for the night Now hammocks were hung from the ceiling, maybe 100 in the room, maybe more, I cannot remember, but they were all touching one another, and keeping in mind that none of us had possibly ever slept in a hammock. It was bound to be somewhat hilarious. Lads were getting in one side, and falling out the other, but eventually, with help from one another, everyone eventually managed to settle into their hammock. Although we were still in dock, and not at sea, there was still a slight movement from the water, and all hammocks swung together, as the ship rocked slightly. God only knows what they would be like when we were out at sea ... we were yet to find out. That night, the ship was due to sail, so by the following morning, we should have been well out to sea.

In the morning, we woke early, looked out of the portholes, only to find that we were still tied up in port! An early announcement was made before breakfast, that the ship would not be leaving that day as there were certain technical problems, so we would be given a 24 hour leave.

Hammocks were stowed away, and we proceeded to collect our breakfast from the cook's galley, and bring it back to the tables and benches underneath where our hammocks had been. Breakfast was not that enjoyable as the stink of sweaty bodies, feet and anything else was quite unbearable and the total lack of ventilation, which was more than necessary when there were in excess of 100 people sleeping in a confined space. Would we get used to it? We had six weeks to try.

Home once again very unexpectedly, and very much a surprise to the family. Once again, time passed quickly and then we were back on board the ship, bound for Singapore. Now the reason we were all sent home, on the grounds of a technical problem, was somewhat more than a general technical problem. We soon learned that the main propeller had dropped off, and gone to the bottom of the dock! So much for the British troop ships! It did appear that so many of these ships did continually have problems of various types, but supposedly, it was due to the fact that most of them were old ships going back to pre-Second World War, and in many cases, before the First World War Hitler was having his revenge. Divers had to be called, along with special equipment, to recover it, and refit it, and finally test it, before the ship could even think of leaving port. Better perhaps that it had happened in port rather than when we were many miles out at sea, and far from a port.

The Empress of Australia left Liverpool on 7<sup>th</sup> December, 1951, to much cheering, and a loud blast from her, to say that she was on her way. The following morning, after breakfast, there was a parade, or muster, as it was sometimes called, on the main deck. Everyone was lined up in a neat regimental formation of rows, and the sergeant major was striding up and down the deck, somewhat irate, for very high up on one of the ships masts, flying in the morning breeze, was a pair of ladies army regulation knickers. He demanded that the person who had put them there should climb up, and get them down!

It was quite obvious that nobody was going to own up to such a prank, and quite a few giggles and laughter broke out, much to the annoyance of sergeant major. It would certainly appear from the height of the knickers that it would not have been a soldier, that would have had the nerve to climb to such a height, and it must also have been during the night, or very early morning, so could only be assumed that it was a member of the ship's crew. The parade was duly dismissed. I think that at some time, that day, the knickers were recovered, as on subsequent mornings there was no sign of them.

The rules for an emergency were carried out, and that of abandon ship, with life jackets being donned, and clear instructions as to which life boat or boats we would use. The ship was slowly making her way down the Irish Sea, and the Celtic Sea, and later would enter the Bay of Biscay. It was not long before the ship started to lurch from side to side, and up and down, which indicated to everyone that we were possibly going to have a rough ride for most of the next day or two. After all, it was winter time, and the seas can get extremely rough. Sickness was everywhere, keeping in mind that it was possibly the first time ever, that most of the passengers had ever been to sea. Below decks, soldiers were retching, and many looking as if they would die. I ventured into one of the large toilet blocks, as I was not feeling too great myself. There were rows of toilets, and these toilet doors were banging open and closed as the ship rolled. It appeared that as the waves hit the side of the ship water and everything came up and out of the toilet pans, covering the floor, which added not only danger to those trying to move, but also to the filth and stench.

How long that lasted, I cannot remember but eventually we passed through the Straits of Gibraltar, where we would see the Rock and into the Mediterranean Sea. Life after that became much more pleasant and calm and sickness subsided completely as everyone got used to the dipping and swaying of the ship.

Being a military troop ship, certain regulations applied, and certain practises were carried out and one of those was that patrols were on duty every night armed with pick axe handles, which perhaps was the standard equipment for this type of patrol. It was possibly thought that if anyone tried to board the ship during the night, clubbing them to death with a pick axe handle was a better option than shooting them, and disturbing everybody's sleep!

As explained earlier, fraternisation of the male troops, with members of the opposite sex, i.e. Queen Alexandra's nurses was strictly forbidden, and the ship was more or less divided into two parts, men at one end, women at the other. I had to perform a night patrol guard duty, and this lasted with so many hours on duty, and so many off. The life boats, were all covered with black tarpaulins, and lined each side of the ship, and as I slowly proceeded past a lifeboat, I could hear the faint giggle of a female or muted conversation between a man and a woman, so it did appear that some of the lads and lasses had broken the rules, but it was most likely members of the crew who had access to all parts of the ship. Being diplomatic, I did not pose any questions to those in the lifeboats or attempt to lift the tarpaulins!

**Empress of Australia in Port Algiers,
me in the foreground.**

Days got brighter, and morning parades, chores and leisure times were quite enjoyable, often spent. looking for whales, or watching the odd dolphin that would swim alongside the ship. We did have physical training almost every other day, and certain drills to do. We were passing along the coast of Morocco, and then Algeria, when there was an announcement over the ship's tannoy system, that the French Foreign Legion based in Algiers, had invited the ship to dock at Algiers, and for everyone to spend the day with them, as fellow soldiers. This was a most welcome invitation, and the ship's reply was that we would be delighted to spend the day with them, at their camp, or in the town. Now we were also clearly informed that the Kasbah in Algiers was an extremely dangerous place to go to, and in fact, our own military police would be on duty there, to ensure that we did not venture to that part of Algiers. It was said that it was a strong Arab quarter, and generally the Arabs did not particularity like westerners, and particularly soldiers. If you went in the chances were that you would not come out! We had to stick to West Algiers, which in fact was a modern city of its day. Merlin, Gerry and I looked around Algiers, and also spent a short time at the Foreign Legion HQ, enjoying a beer or two. Mutual admiration passed between us, which was possibly down to the drink, but we found that the majority of Legionnaires that we spoke to, were not French, but German, Spanish, English and even Polish, plus several other nationalities ... but they all had one thing in common ... they all liked the beer!

What we did not know at that time was that there was a lot of Algerian resistance to the French and their Foreign Legion, and it would be only a couple of years or so later in 1954 that there would be a great uprising against the French rule. So much anti feeling was already there, towards anyone of western origin.

The ship sailed away that late afternoon, heading for the Suez Canal, passing Malta and Crete, en route. The days were warm and pleasant, and shorts were the order of the day. Much time was spent marvelling at the vast ocean, and sea life, all so wondrous for most of us, and a real education. Evenings for most of us were spent playing "Housey Housey", which in modern parlance is "Bingo". I met up with a lad who had a bright idea, that if we purchased a whole sheet of numbers, instead of the half sheet that was the norm, we would between us always have all the numbers on every call. Now whilst there was no guarantee of a win with his scheme it was perhaps comforting to know that every number called, we would have it, and if one of us was doing very badly, we would know that the other was doing extremely well. Strange though it was, we in fact did win several times over the weeks.

**"Bum Boats" alongside ship in Port Said**

Now what is important to know at this point, is that Egypt was at war with Britain in 1951. British service families were being evacuated from the Canal Zone town of Ismailia. Tensions had been very high since the government in Cairo had stepped up its demand for the complete withdrawal of British troops. 6,000 British had been sent to Egypt including the 1$^{st}$ Infantry Division to Fayid in the Central Canal Zone. The 3$^{rd}$ Battalion of the Coldstream Guards from Tripoli in Libya were also brought in to try and quell the riots and anti-British disturbances in the area. The 3$^{rd}$ Battalion of the Grenadier Guards, plus the 1$^{st}$ Battalion of the Cameron Highlanders were also called upon.

In October 1951, Egypt had denounced the Anglo Egyptian 1936 Treaty, so things in the area of the Suez Canal which we were approaching, was not looking too good to say the least.

Fortunately, the British had taken over complete control of the Suez Canal, and the whole Canal Zone. Egyptian workers had downed tools completely at Port Said, Port Foud, and

Suez, but the British had enough manpower and expertise to keep everything running as normally as possible.

Our ship entered the canal during this emergency. Guns were all manned on deck, and troops were told to keep a very low profile, as the ship proceeded along the canal. On route down the canal at various locations were Arab men who knowing that our ship was British, lifted their galabeyas (long shirt) and made various rude gestures, which really did not cause any real problems for the troops aboard, but may have offended, or maybe pleased, or amused the females aboard the ship.

The canal is perhaps longer than one realises, at 163 kilometres, and about 60 metres wide at its very narrowest point. Port Said, and Port Foud are at the northern end, then Qantara, both east and west banks of the canal. Ismailia the main town, then to the Great Bitter Lakes, where the R.A.F. had a base, then Port Tawfiq, Suez, then out into the Gulf of Aden.

The ship was now out into open waters, and heading for the next destination, which would be the Yemen, and the port of Aden. Now to give it its correct name, it was the Aden Protectorate. Conquered by Great Britain in 1839 and the British wanted to colonise the whole of southern Yemen. British influence, however, did extend, right to Hadhramaut by the 1950s, and in fact that did continue, right through until the 1960s.

Aden was protected by a unit of the Aden Protectorate Levite troops which were basically colonial troops responsible for the defence of Aden. There was sporadic fighting in 1952 ... but much of this was after our visit to the port!

**Myself with Merlin Rhodes in Aden**

The Empress of Australia steamed into Aden, to refuel, and to replenish certain supplies. When docked, we were able to disembark and have a look around. What a filthy backward place it was, with Arabs poorly dressed, many with clothes that were soiled, and filthy, with that furtive look that many had, and perhaps particularly at the site of British soldiers, who were not their greatest friends. Cows and goats were wandering the streets, some lying in the roadway and others just depositing their toilets, wherever they chose. The odd cow, wandering into one of the open shop fronts, to be chased out by the owner, hitting the animal, with a stick, that he obviously kept close at hand, for that particular purpose. Many of the buildings were dirty, grimed, and with plaster falling off the walls, looking as though they could collapse at any moment. Welcome to the Arab world! We did feel rather sorry for those stationed there. There was in port a cargo ship, the "Kabyle," being loaded with oranges. Not just a box or two, but thousands of boxes, and we wondered if they were destined for the UK, or some other European port. Before long the ship finally sailed, and everyone was on board, "bum boats" appeared alongside the ship, trying to sell all manner of things, with the usual skills of these Arabs passing goods up to you on ropes, and you passing money down to them on ropes. Nevertheless, it was quite obvious from the number of ships in port, loading and unloading merchandise of every description, that Aden was an extremely important destination in the maritime world.

Moving away from Aden, we were soon into the Arabian Sea, and on to our next destination, which would be Colombo, in Ceylon. We had one day to spend in Colombo, and found that it was a most pleasant town compared to what we had left behind at our last port of call. Buildings were clean, people were smiling, and happy, and spoke to you. The three of us, Gerry, Merlin and me had a good look around and could not resist the enormous, sweet pineapples that were being offered by street traders, so we made a few purchases to take back to the ship. We found a place also that we could have a drink and a snack. It was a Seaman's Rest, which we later learned could often be found in most of the later ports of the East and Far East and which were often run by a Christian Church organisation. As sailors from around the world were working on the many cargo ships, it was somewhere that they could rest, have food, and converse with other sailors from many countries of the world. There was often a chaplain working there, who could give advice and comfort to those that needed him, regardless of their particular religion.

Now exactly where the ship was positioned for Christmas Day, I cannot actually remember, which is rather remiss of me, but Christmas 1951 was certainly a day to remember for the rest of my life. It is totally amazing to think what a wonderful lunch we had on board, and all served by officers, as was military tradition. I am not 100% sure that our menu was exactly the same, and as comprehensive as that of the officers, wives and nursing corps, but regardless of that, and to think that it had all been produced in the kitchens on board, by the naval cooks or the Army Catering Corps cooks, it was a wonderful achievement. Cooking for at least 2,000 troops, officers, wives, and nurses, plus crew, one must be talking about 2,000 in all ... big congratulations all round! Luckily an original menu was recovered, and here it is:

**XMAS DAY 1951**
**The Seasons Greeting**
**The Captain, Officers and Crew, wish you a**
**VERY HAPPY CHRISTMAS**

**MENU**

**Consommé Royale Cream of Tomato Velour**
**Fried Fillet of Plaice, sauce tartar**
**Roast young Turkey, sprouts au beurre**
**Parsilles and croquette potatoes**

**COLD**

**Pressed Ox Tongue**
**Salade Beaucaire**

**English Plum pudding, rum sauce**
**Vanilla ice cream with wafers**
**Mince pies Xmas cake**
**Dessert coffee**

**S.S. EMPRESS of AUSTRALIA**
**XMAS 1951**

**Government Building, Singapore**

Arrival in Singapore, and much movement of shipping, in this great and important Far Eastern port, Cargo, passenger ferry boats, and ships, many from Hong Kong, China, Japan and other Far Eastern destinations, and the sound of cranes loading, unloading, and the general chatter, and shouting of dockers and crew members.

With our ship well secured there was much activity, with military personnel all over the docks, embarking from the Empress of Australia, and over the heads of many, swung the great nets, full of goods, which were lowered onto the dockside to be swiftly emptied, and returned onto the ship.

We did learn that our ship had not reached her final destination, but would be going on to Pusan, in Korea, to allow more troops to disembark and to pick up others that were returning from the Korean War.

We were duly instructed and guided ashore, carrying our kitbags. Quickly and efficiently our details were checked by certain military waiting at the dockside. Merlin, Gerry and I were still together, solely down to our names being in that alphabetical order, Preston, Rhodes and Richards. The three of us were issued each with .303 rifles, and a cotton belt, with pockets, containing ammunition for our rifles. We were issued with railway tickets for a place called Tampin, which we had never heard of, and not a clue where it was, apart from the fact that it was somewhere up country, in Malaya. The seats were wooden slatted seats, and there were civilian passengers on the train, some with children. Obviously of different ethnic origin, but their looks were Indian, Chinese, Malay, but they were all residents of Malaya. One could converse with some of them as English was a language which most of them understood and perhaps even spoke. Not necessarily that fluently in English, but a lot better than our Malay which was nil. This was quite a bonus for us.

The train was slow, stopping and starting, and belching smoke, not only upwards, but often into the open carriage windows. As the ulu, or jungle vegetation was so close to the railway line, one could now easily understand how easy it was for the "bandits" as we called them, to lie in wait and attack a train, either by derailing it, blowing up the train, or even climbing aboard and attacking passengers, when the train slowed down, on tackling an incline. Once again we stopped in a siding, whilst another train on the main track, going south, passed by. The problem was that it was a single line, despite the fact that it was a main line, feeding from Singapore to Ipoh, and maybe beyond. Once again, a shrill blast from the train's whistle, and we were off again. The "clickety-click" of the train wheels at every join in the rails continued for some time, until we arrived at Tampin station. A clean, neat station, and clearly marked with the station's name on a large board.

We bid farewell to our fellow passengers, and wave to the children, and we were now in Negri Sembilan, a state of Malaya. We proceeded to the road, with kitbag and rifle, and looked around, but nothing there at all. In fact the road both ways was totally empty, we had a somewhat chilling feeling, thinking about the atrocities which had been, and were carried out by the communist guerrillas (bandits).

**Two Malay Policemen**

Then, quite suddenly, there appeared a large army lorry coming towards us, and started to turn around right next to us. We asked if he had come to pick us up, but he said he hadn't and it was only by chance, he had seen us. We climbed aboard for the trip to the army camp just outside of the village of Tampin. We say, "Village" as we did not know if it was a village or town. Soon the driver turned off the tarmac road, onto a rough, dusty track, which led to the camp. We had passed a farmer on the way, ploughing with a water buffalo, and single furrow plough, and two Tamil women, who we later learned were rubber tappers, working on a local plantation.

The camp consisted of a few Bashas (traditional wooden framed hut, with various leaves for roof and sides), plus a number of tents and the camp's main office. We were ushered into the office where we presented our documentation to the duty officer, who read them carefully, and then declared that they were not expecting us, and did not have a clue where we should have been posted, but they would contact the powers that be, in Singapore, and find out. Meanwhile we were to spend our time at their camp. Now there were two Scottish regiments there, and I cannot be 100% sure, but I think that one was the Cameronians, and the other the Gordon Highlanders. I did not consider that they were the Argyle & Sutherland Highlanders, as I am sure that most of these lads were from somewhere in Scotland, because of their broad accents, laughter, and general antics. A good crowd to be with, and far better that they were on our side than the other side, as the Scots have always been great, brave, and fierce fighters, as history has told us from the past battles on home soil.

And not forgetting the famous old regiment, the Green Howards, they were there as well.

For almost a week we were non-existent and were able to spend most days on our own, wandering the camp and finding out what facilities they had, including a trip into Tampin. Yes it could be classified as a town, and had the usual hustle and bustle that went with such Malayan towns and villages, as we learned. A smell of food wafted through the area, along with other smells which we became used to in our future time in Malaya.

The three of us were eventually called into the camp office and informed that Singapore had now informed them of our true postings. We were all to be sent in different directions, and every one would be a surprise. One was to go to a Malay regiment, and one to an artillery regiment and myself to the 22$^{nd}$ Gurkha Rifles (Sirmoor Rifles), a very old and honourable regiment ... how lucky could I be! As a boy, I had heard about the Gurkhas, and their bravery, fighting many battles all over the world, and particularly their bravery in recent years.

Saying our farewells was quite something, keeping in mind that we three had been together for such a long period of time, and did not expect that we would ever meet up again. I was to head for the town of Ipoh, a large town that had many different regiments based there, and an enormous camp, or camps, situated within the area of Ipoh. There were Lancers, Hussars, Commandos, Gurkhas, in fact far too many to ever remember.

On arrival there, I was directed to a building which was for the 48 Gurkha brigade, and was ushered into a room, where the commanding officer of the 22$^{nd}$ Gurkha Rifles resided. His name was Lt. Col. Cruickshank, and what a charming man he was. He welcomed me to the regiment, and informed me that he had spent some twenty five or thirty years with the Gurkhas, fighting up on the north west frontier the Khyber Pass, and many other destinations, many of which I had heard about, or read about, but did not necessarily know in exactly which part of the world they were. Lt. Col. Cruickshank obviously spoke fluent Nepali or Gurkhali as it is sometimes called. It is a language not too dissimilar to the Indian Hindi language. He said to me "Richards, I will give you three pieces of advice, which is very worthwhile advice, based upon my years of experience with the Gurkhas. One is to learn their language, two is to eat their food, and three is to respect their religion, and you will never have a better friend in the world than a Gurkha. I wish you well." I was dismissed with a handshake! I thought to myself, what a fantastic and warm-hearted man, and what a fantastic piece of advice, which I have never forgotten.

I was sent to "B" company of the 22$^{nd}$ Gurkhas, who were stationed at Slim River. I was soon introduced to a few of the men there, including Jock Thompson a REME man, plus one or two Gurkhas. I was also issued with a Gurkha Kukri, which was a great surprise, not being a Gurkha, but it was something I cherished, and was very proud to have.

Now there were many, many trouble spots throughout Malaya, and Slim River was perhaps one of them. Disruptions caused by the bandits (communist guerrillas), intimidation of men and women living in small enclaves on the edge of the jungle (ulu) where people had been tortured, killed, and mutilated, with their bodies being left in places where others would see them, and this gave out a very stark warning to others, to co-operate with the bandits, and to give them food, and anything else they required. Slim River was in the state of

Perak, situated north of Kuala Lumpur, by about 100 km. It sat by the Sungai Slim (sungai, meaning river, in Malay).

Going back to the time of the Japanese invasion of Malaya, there had been a ferocious battle at Slim River, between the Imperial Japanese Army and the British Indian Arms. The 2nd Indian Brigade was practically annihilated at Slim River, so we were in an area of some notability.

Now just before I proceed further, I would like to revert to the Gurkha Kukri, which I now proudly possessed. As most people know, this is the well-known Gurkha knife, but there are several misconceptions, about it. Firstly it is made from quality steel, and heavily weighted from its tip, to its curve. It gives added speed to the force of the blow delivered. The tiny niches just a short distance from the handle are not sights for throwing, as the knife is never thrown, but is so that blood can drip away from the blade, without getting onto the handle. The handle is often made from bone, or synthetic material. With regard to a Gurkha always having to draw blood, if he takes his kukri from its scabbard ... this I have never witnessed in all my time with them. There are also two smaller knives within the scabbard, one a sharpening knife, the other a skinning knife. The scabbard is usually attached to the waist belt on the left hand side, so easily removing the kukri, with the right hand.

**Myself with Jeep Ambulance at Slim River**

There was a single railway track running down from the
north of Malaya, down to Singapore, with many passing points
at intervals along the line, so that trains going in either
direction could pass one another, and Slim River station was
close to camp. One of the biggest problems facing Malayan
Railways was the constant efforts of the bandits to blow up the
tracks, on whatever line they could, causing the maximum
amount of mayhem, and possibly loss of life. One of the
answers to this problem was to patrol sections of the line, prior
to a train emerging. The British Army, in conjunction with the
railway authorities had devised a novel way of doing this. An
army jeep, with its wheels removed, and with axles, and train
wheels fitted. This was used from time to time, by railway
inspectors to check the condition of track and points, but the
army jeep could be armed with two searchlights, and Bren gun,
plus four armed soldiers. Steering wheel was obviously of no
use, and all the driver had to do was drive normally, and
change gear!

This was a regular mission which took place several times a week, and during the daytime was quite an exciting experience, but still keeping in mind that fifteen minutes or so behind you was a train of several tons!

The jeep was driven along the line until it was decided that the particular stretch of line had been completed, and one of the railway staff would operate a lever, changing the points, so that you would run into a siding, and once in, points changed back to main line. This was normally, the distance between two stations that were patrolled.

**Rail Line Checking with Converted Jeep**

I only engaged in an evening outing once in the jeep, and must admit that it was somewhat scary, as the searchlights are switched on, and you sweep from left to right of the track with them. Sometimes you think you have seen things, that are not actually there, but also have the worrying thought of the train bearing down the track, not that far behind you.

Why did I get involved in such a mission? The reason was that the jeep had from time to time had engine problems, in that it was miss-firing. Now that can be dangerous, in that one could not afford to have a breakdown with the jeep ... far too dangerous, and very much exposed to the enemy if they happened to be in the area. I, fortunately, was able to sort out the problem, and really needed to be in the jeep, so that I could listen to the engine, and make sure that I had corrected the fault. As a non-combatant soldier, I really should not have travelled in that jeep ... but at least from another point of view, and because of the mechanical side of it I was not too much out of order.

Only on one daytime trip, did we come across a small group, gathered around one point of the track, and we opened fire, upon which they immediately scattered, without returning fire. No one was hit. We stopped at that very point and inspected the track, but there was no sign of damage, or of anything there, to cause damage, so perhaps we had arrived just in time, and we then moved on quickly.

It was quite obvious that this particular method of checking the railway track, was certainly not the best method, but at that particular time, there was no alternative, despite the fact that it was a dangerous outing, with no armour whatsoever, to protect the vehicle or occupants. This matter had been brought to the attention of the military, the police and other serving groups in Malaya, so in late 1951/52, a very large English company, specialising in the manufacture of railway carriages, trolleys and the like, were approached to come up with an answer to the problem. The name of the company was D. Wickham & Co., based in Ware, Hertfordshire. They had a very large factory there, and a foundry. They manufactured various rail carriages, carts, trolleys, and exported throughout the world, including the home market of the UK.

They came up with the Wickham Armoured Railcar, 42 of which were delivered to Malayan railways in 1953. It was fully armoured, with an unladen weight of 6.75 tons, self-propelled and could carry six men These were used mainly by the

Malayan police force, and became an important part of the fight against derailment of trains throughout Malaya.

**Rubber Plantation Armoured Car for Malay Police**

Whilst in Malaya, I did learn that a distant relation of the family was in fact a manager of a rubber plantation, the Perhensian Tinggi Rubber Estate, not far from Seremban, and so whilst I was in that area, I decided to make contact with him, and his family. With permission, I took an army vehicle, a Humber Scout car to be precise, and drove myself, without a gunner on top, which would have been the norm, to the estate. At the entry to the estate, there were four armed Malay police, which were part of the allocation of police designated to look after the family. This was a normal procedure on all rubber estates, as all managers, and their families were always prime targets for the communist bandits. Chin Peng, their leader realised that continual intimidation would result in the closing down of an estate, and loss of revenue to its British owners. Every estate had its own armoured vehicle to try and protect the rubber planter and his family, and wherever they went, they almost always went with armed police protection.

Now the Malay police recognising the army scout car, with its $2/2^{nd}$ insignia, emblazoned on the front of the vehicle, did not hesitate to allow me through. I was greeted by this jovial man, a distant relation that I had never met before and introduced to his wife and children. I spent a pleasant afternoon with them, but during which time, I realised what a difficult and dangerous life they led. Attacks upon their property happened regularly, and only a week ago, the children had been playing in the garden, when, without any prior warning a hail of bullets passed over their heads from a terrorist group. Malay police immediately returned fire, whilst ushering the children to safety of the house.

On my eventual return to the UK, I did learn that he had been killed by the bandits, and his wife and children had returned to the safety of the UK.

It is perhaps very important at this stage, to mention two of the most important men, so very much involved in the eventual downfall of the communist insurgency in Malaya. One was Sir Gerald Templar, whom I had the pleasure of meeting later on in my time in Malaya, and that I will tell you about, at a later time. Field Marshall Sir Gerald Templar was his full title, and he had replaced the previous High Commissioner of Malaya, Sir Henry Lovell Goldsworthy Gurney, who was killed in an ambush on $6^{th}$ October, 1951. Sir Gerald Templar was a military commander who fought in two world wars, and was appointed as British High Commissioner in Malaya, on the $22^{nd}$ of January, 1952, by Sir Winston Churchill, and he remained in that position until 1954. His idea was not just to get more troops into the jungle, but to win the hearts and minds of the Malaysian people, by constructing new villages, better water, and other facilities, and by this method, things did improve dramatically.

The other man of such great importance was a retired British Army officer, who had in fact retired back in 1949. His name, Lieutenant General Sir Harold Briggs was brought in as the Army's Director of Operations, in Malaya, and in June 1950, he introduced the Briggs Plan.

This was a resettlement plan for around 500,000 Malays to relocate from squatter communities on the fringe of forests and jungle, to guarded camps or New Villages as they were often called. Briggs could see that an important part of beating the bandits was to deprive them of food, and supplies which local squatters living in such outlying and remote areas, had been forced to supply, under dreadful threats of torture and death, if they did not comply. Not everyone was keen on the idea of relocating, but the majority were.

In addition to the 5,000 to 8,000 armed bandits fighting in the jungle, against British and Commonwealth troops, there were also some 1,500 to 2,000 Min Yuen. Now these were basically of Chinese ethnic origin, who supported the communists and a very high percentage of them were also armed. It was a people's movement, who supported the bandits in a very useful way. Many of these were also forced to relocate, and although they were not always easily identifiable, would now find it extremely difficult to operate, living within a new village, and in most cases would make it impossible, with checks at the gates of villages, with armed police guards or soldiers of the Malay Regiment, checking all moves in and out of the village.

Deep penetration was also increased into the jungle, particularly the remote parts. SAS and Australian infantry were expert in coping with the dense jungle terrain and could survive up to around 40 or 45 days with supplies dropped by air, to them. Other pressure was put upon the bandits by our troops being deposited onto the ground unexpectedly, by Western helicopters, in all sorts of areas and by scaling down ropes into limited spaces. Sikorsky Whirlwind helicopters from Naval Air Squadron of the Fleet Air Arm could also drop troops very accurately into specially prepared areas of jungle clearing, which had been prepared by ground troops, specialising in this type of work.

During my time in Malaya, I obviously came across many other soldiers, from many different countries, and particularly on the occasions that I returned from time to time to the HQ of 48 Gurkha Brigade in Ipoh.

The main NAAFI there was a very large complex, where many would gather, to eat, to drink, and to have a chat with others, discussing what they had done, what letters they had received from home, and the general conversations that you would expect.

**Artillery in Action, 25 Pound Gun**

Every one of the regiments involved played such an important part in the eventual defeat of the communist guerrillas, so that nobody could ever pick out one regiment or battalion, as the best, because that would be so unfair. Granted that there were those who were having a great deal of luck at a particular moment, as that is the way things go. Suddenly jungle patrols in the right area, at the right time, and able to strike hard, and make a good number of kills. The Glorious Glosters seemed to be having that luck at one time, I remember.

Take for instance, the Fiji Battalion, commanded by Sir Edward Cakobau, who later became Prime Minister of Fiji. They served from 1952, until 1956, a total of 1,600 men. Sadly, some were killed in combat within a few weeks of their arrival. Mistakes in the early part of a company's first operations could easily be made, because jungle warfare, including the penetration into rubber plantations, was a very difficult, and exacting type of engagement, and not like any other which had possibly been experienced.

That is why one can only speak so highly of the National Servicemen, who adapted so quickly to such difficult conditions of heat swamps, midges, and all the nasty things that can be found in the jungle, and never had a prior opportunity back in the UK to experience anything like it.

The Royal Regiment of Artillery had a very long and important role in the 1950s in Malay. Also the 25th field regiment were also involved. There were about five field regiments, plus three field batteries. Whilst the 2/2nd Gurkhas only had the small support artillery of 17poinder guns, like many regiments they were really not up to what was required, and not able to inflict sufficient damage upon the enemy. In real terms, they were only able to make a few "Pot holes"! The Royal Artillery had the 25 pounder guns, and perhaps even the 5.5 guns, which were up to the tasks demanded, These 25 pounders had the explosive power to uproot trees, to fell trees, breaking them in half causing serious problems on the ground for the guerrillas, and with the constant bombarding over a period of a few hours, intermittent or not, it could cause extensive disarray to the guerrillas, particularly if the gun-layers had their targets, spot on, from the information given, so that the shells actually fell upon a guerrilla encampment!

There were certain times when there would be a large concerted effort to attack a known area where bandits were hiding out, in large numbers. Such operations would be coordinated, with several infantry regiments, and to bombard the area with artillery, before an advance sweep through the jungle, was of prime importance. The artillery could then at a given notification, re-calibrate their guns, so that the shells would drop another few hundred yards or a quarter of a mile ahead of the last bombardment. Such an operation was performed whilst I was in Malaya, upon the Blue Valley, but I never did learn or know, exactly where the Blue Valley was!

It must also be remembered that the Royal Navy could be of invaluable assistance in this type of operation, as they could fire shells whilst sitting just off the coast and their navel guns could inflict untold damage upon a bandit infested area. Between actual firing, spotter planes could report damage, and assist greatly in precisely directing those artillery men.

As far as the infantry were concerned, there were so many historic regiments engaged, that it would be totally unfair to select any one regiment or battalion for special praise. There was great competition between infantry and that was to see who had gained the greatest number of kills, and almost daily, news would come through that such and such a company had killed a well-known bandit, and several of his fellow bandits.

When a patrol was to go out, and into the jungle for a few days, as explained before, they were usually taken by road to a given spot, maybe only a short distance away from camp, or maybe a lengthier journey of a few miles. This was usually the job of a Gurkha driver, sometimes escorted, and sometimes not, depending on the terrain, the remoteness, and other factors which would be dangerous.

So I did not always take them out, as my main job was to ensure that our vehicles were running and roadworthy, maintaining the vehicles with my colleagues.

On most occasions when a vehicle returned, it had only collected the returning patrol, but there were other occasions, where they had made a kill, or maybe two, and brought back the dead bandits, which would be eventually deposited, possibly at the local police station, and placed on public display. This would be very much dependant on the condition of the body. I rarely had the desire to peer into the back of the returning lorry, even though the word had quickly buzzed around the camp, that the patrol had experienced a successful few days in the jungle.

However, there was one particular occasion, when I learned that the patrol had killed, and brought back a female bandit. Now whilst there were a great number of female terrorists fighting with their male counterparts, the curiosity got the better of me, as I had never witnessed a dead female terrorist. Perhaps this was a sordid or depraved part of my mind, which had overcome me, and was not just curiosity ... this strange desire to see such a ghoulish thing!

I climbed up the side of the open lorry, peering into it, with some nervous in trepidation. Perhaps at that moment, I wished that I had not been so curious, as there, still tied to the bamboo pole, on which they had carried her was this Chinese girl; possibly not more than seventeen or eighteen years of age, dressed in the standard outfit of the communist bandits. Dirty beige trousers and jacket, cloth puttees, partially unwound, and hanging over her boots, thick with mud and soaking wet, as was most of her clothing. She was face upwards, with pale skin, spattered with blood, where the bullets, obviously from some automatic weapon, had cut across her breasts, and left shoulder, leaving quite a substantial open wound. Her dark black hair was very much of a masculine style, and she could have been taken for a man quite easily.

It was pretty obvious from the type of frontal wound that it must have been a very quick and unexpected confrontation, suggestion that she may have been a "Lookout" for other comrades gathered back some distance away, maybe even resting. She had been unceremoniously thrown into the back of the lorry, along with her weapon, which looked like a Lee Enfield No 4 Rifle. No match for what the Gurkha patrol could offer!

I was partly shocked, and stunned, to see this young girl, her life taken from her at such an early age and in such a callous and sad way. Someone's daughter, someone's girlfriend, who would never see her again. A young person, so ill-informed and so misguided in her aim in life about something which would never come to fruition. This was not an appropriate time for my beloved camera, but a time for compassion!

The demand of continual movement of troops during the Malayan Emergency was quite considerable, and this was quite normal, as troops suddenly had to move to link up with others on special operations. Certain specialist troops were used, where special needs were, and in the comparatively short time that I was in Malaya, I have really lost count of the number of towns and villages, that we were either encamped at, or passed through, in the course of operations. Kluang, in Jahore, Tana Rata, Ipoh, Taiping, Tronah, Kulai, Tapah, Kuala Lipis, Sungei Patani, in the state if Pahang, Kelang, or Klang as it is sometimes known, in Selangor state. Tanjong Malim, Kuala Kansar, Seremban, and these are just a few that are remembered. One particular instance does however stand out very clearly in my mind, and that was when a contingent of "B" company, were to go on a trek, quite a long way from camp, and which would take us away for several days. I was to go with them, and as a REME man it would be my responsibility to provide lighting, when and where, it might be needed, so I had to take with me a large, petrol-driven generator which my vehicle would tow with miles of lighting cable, and lots of bulbs. We travelled in an armed convoy, with the usual scout car to the front, and another at the rear, which was the normal procedure, and leading this expedition was none other than Lt. Col. Cruikshank. As we proceeded through roads, none of which I recognised, and on a route with which I was not familiar, with thick jungle either side of the roads, and with no civilisation to witness, we suddenly came upon what can only be called a totally deserted village, which consisted of about six brick built properties on either side of the road. It had obviously been deserted for some considerable time as most of the roofs had collapsed, and parts of walls had broken inwards or outwards, leaving great gaps, in each building.

**Yours Truly on Lt. Cruickshank's Trip!**

It was here that the colonel decided was a suitable place to stop for the night, and make camp. The colonel asked me if it would be possible for me to rig up a complete lighting system, on both sides of the road, and into each building, or what was left of the buildings. With the help of my dear Gurkha friends, they managed to chop down some very long lengths of bamboo, sufficiently long enough that we could lift the wiring up to a sufficient height to go from one side of the road to the other, and at a height that would be higher than any vehicle that would ever pass this way, although none was expected, or likely. We did smash down some further sections of walls to enable us to feed the wiring through to each. Now this cabling was quite a clever invention. The cable being totally flat, and the bulbs already each fitted into a socket. On the end of the socket were two protruding metal spikes, slightly offset, with a space to place the flat cable, and a further piece of socket. You pressed the bulb socket onto the cable, where the two offset spikes engaged into the flat wire, and you then screwed on the other piece of socket, a perfect connection every time.

Now was a slightly worrying moment, the moment of truth. Sometimes these army generators were extremely difficult to start, so I hoped for the best. A few strong winds of the handle, and the generator fired into life, and within seconds it settled down to that regular beat, which told me that everything would be ok. This little deserted and derelict village, in the middle of nowhere, had become akin to Piccadilly Circus, lighting up the jungle. The usual great cheer went up, as a sign of joy and approval.

Meanwhile the Gurkha cooks had made a wonderful fire, which crackled as the wood and bamboo burned. It did appear that our commanding officer had decided that we were too strong, and too well armed for any bandits to attack us, despite the fact, that we were so obvious, even to the animals in the jungle.

The colonel did say to me ... "Well done Richards" and was obviously impressed with the ability of the REME, so much that he actually invited me to share a meal with him. How could I refuse!

Having accepted his invitation, we both sat down on a couple of ammunition boxes, which were readily available, and opened up our ration packs, which in fact were quite adequate, and enjoyable. Hot sweet tea was provided by a Gurkha cook, which he had brewed upon the open fire. The conversation between the colonel and myself, was somewhat akin to a questionnaire, but not knowing one another sufficiently, that was not surprising He asked me where I lived in civvy street, where I had gone to school, and where I worked and what I was training for. I in return was able to ask him how long he had served with the Gurkhas, and what theatres of war he had been in, and that was most interesting. During the evening the colonel produced four bottles of "Tiger beer," which was very civil of him, and came as a nice surprise. Two bottles each, before bedtime.

Time came around for bed, and I bedded down with my fellow Gurkhas, for the night, and quite obviously a guard had been arranged for the duration of the night, with about eight of the Gurkhas dotted around, and just on the outskirts of our "village", so everyone could sleep without worry.

The following morning everyone was awake early, and all washing as best we could with the very limited amount of water we had. Each had just about enough to clean teeth, and splash your face. Toilets were squat wherever you could; just a few yards away from the "village", but still had the assurance of guards being in close proximity to you.

The sound of jungle birds is always pleasing, and now and again the chatter of monkeys. The two Ghurkha cooks were actually preparing some curried vegetables with dal and rice, plus the emphatic mug of hot sweet tea. Whilst all of that was being prepared, myself, along with half a dozen Ghurkhas were dismantling the wiring, rolling it up, and stowing it away. We were now on our way once again, and had only covered a few miles, when we came upon a small group of Sakai men and women. We stopped, and asked them if they were ok. We also found out where they were from, and found out that they were more or less within a few hundred yards of their village. By pointing into the jungle, which at that point was very dense, they indicated the direction, but it was not clearly visible. How we managed to get anything from them I do not know as they really spoke no English. One or two of the Gurkhas had learned a smattering of Malay, but the problem was that they did not speak pure Malay, but a language more or less of their own. For me, all I had learned in Malay was, "Mana pigi la," which is "Where are you going." Not much really in such circumstances. However I was able to get my camera out, and take a few pictures of them, after getting what I hoped had been their permission. Naked to the waist, some with tribal markings, but quite content to have their photos taken. Walking just a few yards up alongside our convoy, there was quite a clearing in the undergrowth, and one could see in the distance where some cultivation had taken place and this was obviously from where they had come.

From seeing where they lived, it was very obvious that the bandits could easily raid such people and their land, and demand fruit and vegetables, and it made one realise how important the job of the government and of the military was to get these people into a much safer environment, and that's what we were here to do.

**Sakai Women**

To my knowledge, during the Malayan Emergency, very few mistakes had been made by the military with regard to their actions and conduct towards local people, and even towards the bandits that had been captured. The British Army along with the Commonwealth, and other troops, police, and all involved had acted in the usual traditions expected of them ... but with one exception, and that was what became to be known as the Batang Kali Massacre. It involved the indiscriminate killing of 24 unarmed civilians (villagers) by British troops on December 12th 1948, 7 platoon, G Company, 2nd Scots Guards, surrounded a rubber plantation at Sungai Rioh, near Batang Kali, in Selangor. The civilians were rounded up. Men were separated from women and children for interrogation. Shooting was then heard. There were a total of 24 unarmed villagers killed, and the village was set on fire. The only male survivor was a man named Chong Hong who was in his twenties at the time. He had fainted and was presumed dead. Other eye witnesses included victim's spouses, and children such as Tha Yong, aged seventeen, and Loh Ah Choy, who was aged seven years. There have been many investigations as to the seriousness, and authenticity of this massacre, judicial equities, and claims against the British government, but sadly nothing has actually been done to bring those responsible to justice, if that was what was needed and the case against them proven.

**Singapore**

Did we have the chance of a holiday whilst in Malaya? Yes, we certainly did, and I took the opportunity to go down to Singapore and have a look around at this most important of Far Eastern cities. I had a week's leave and booked into the Britannia Club, in Beach Road. This was a hotel, for non-commissioned officers, from army, navy, or air force, and was run by the NAAFI and WVS (women's voluntary service.)

Rates were reasonable, rooms satisfactory, and meals available throughout the day, and well into the evenings. At that time, back in the 50s, places such as Sing Beer Bar and restaurant, on Changi Road, offered coffee at 20 cents. Beer was around 60/70 cents depending on the brew, and if you had something quite simple, such as steak, egg, and chips, it would knock you back $1.70., scrambled eggs and chips, cheaper at 90 cents. Tiger beer was a favourite and distributed by a company called Fraser & Neave Ltd.

If there was a downside to the holiday, it was that on arrival at the hotel, I was quite tired, and decided to have a short nap on my bed, but when I woke up; my wallet had been stolen from my pocket, whilst asleep. Must have slept deeper that I intended!

I wore civilian clothes whilst in Singapore, and went to a couple of dance halls. When you entered the place, you would purchase, and pay for a number of tickets. Around the dancing area would be a number of hostesses, so if you wanted to dance you had to choose a hostess, go up to her and give her a ticket. One ticket for each dance. At the end of the evening, the girls would be paid a certain percentage, according to how many dances they had had, and the number of tickets submitted to their manager.

During my leave in Singapore I visited Chinatown, a very busy bustling area, selling every conceivable type of Chinese food in their market, and their busy eating places, with a wonderful aroma, that only Chinese food can produce. But not to be outdone there was another area, which was typically Indian, and once again, wonderful aromas of spices and curries.

The Supreme Court was a very gracious colonial building and the General Post Office, that iconic building to always be remembered. The Keppel Road Railway Station, "Tanjong Pagar" was opened in 1932 by Sir Cecil Cementi, in those days belonging to and part of the Federated Malay States Railways.

As for the Central Fire Station, such an ornate building, and so unique that anyone that has ever seen it, could never forget it! For me, this was all such a wonderful experience, and all at the expense of the British government of the day ... so how lucky could you get?

**Sakai Family, Man has Blow Pipe**

Now I have not mentioned the Sakai people of Malaya. The indigenous people of the original Orange Asil Tribe. These people I came in contact with several times over the period of my time in Malaya. Several times, on special missions, we would come across them.

Northern people which were the Semangs, were often referred to as Sakai, and the Batecks again were an original group or tribe, but they lived mainly in the north of the country, living a very mobile way of life, moving on each day, and not settling in any one particular place.

There were many different tribes in Malaya in the past, and whilst we referred to them as Sakai, this was not meant in any derogatory way. The Sakai, which we met up with on occasions, were basically slim. They lived from mainly berries, nuts, fruit, pith, leaves, shoots and tubers, all readily available in the jungle. They were also involved in hunting and fishing, and their main weapon was the blow pipe.

This pipe was made from a very special quality of bamboo. It was as about six feet or so in length, but sometimes even longer. The arrows used, were tipped with a poisonous resin from the Ipo tree, which was often heard to increase the intensity of the poison content. The men were pretty accurate with these, up to about a maximum distance of thirty yards, and when asked, you could see them dart a monkey at such a height. Clothing was mainly a loin cloth for the men, and sometimes a cloth tied around their head. The women were quite modest, covering their lower parts, with what can only be describe as a skirt, but their breasts were usually uncovered. They spoke in their own tongue, but could usually communicate most things by sign language.

They were friendly people, but one just always respected their way of life, and treated their women most respectfully as one never knew how they would react, and with poison darts, and blowpipes, I always played things very carefully. Their housing was the simple "longhouse" build up on its stilts, and very similar to the Dyaks. The "longhouse" housed two or three families, and so there were good communal relationships and children would always benefit and be looked after by women that were available, whilst others would be involved in gathering vegetables, and cooking. The men appeared to be responsible for the hunting, fishing, building and maintenance of the longhouse, plus collecting of wood, and bamboo for their arrows and blowpipe, and also for other types of wood for burning.

I was fortunate to get photographs of both the men and women plus children, without too much trouble, as one must always be extremely careful when requesting photographs of such native people. Always ask first, before you point a camera at anyone.

Once they have that trust in you they will happily pose for photographs, keep smiling, and chattering away amongst themselves, and this was despite the fact that you were unable to show them the results from your camera immediately, as can be done today.

There is an area in Nepal, known as the Bard District, close to the Indian border, and within that district, a village known as Bariyapur. Once every five years there is a festival, honouring the Hindu goddess, Gladhimai at the Fadhimai Temple.

People travel from all over Nepal, and from many parts of India to witness this festival, which is the worlds' biggest event of animal slaughter. The Hindus sacrifice up to 250,000 animals at this one festival, and all by decapitation. Crowds of men, brandishing enormous Kukri and other knives, can be seen making their way along tracks, and roads to Bariyapur. Animals for slaughter are usually covered with a red cloth of some description, which is the sign for the animal to be slaughtered. Buffalo are herded into pens, as are goats and other animals, many of whom have trekked from long distances. Others which are smaller are carried by their owners to this place of execution.

When the festival gets under way, the blood, the carnage is unbelievable, and very distressful to those not of the Hindu religion. The bellowing of the buffalos, the cries and bleating of the goats, as the butchers hack at the animal's neck. Sometimes death comes quickly with one blow from the executioner, but more often or not, it takes more than one single blow. The ground is deep with blood, heads of decapitated animals, bodies everywhere, and the stench of blood, dung, and all that goes with this mass execution. Some animals, already covered in the blood of others, fear in their eyes awaiting their own execution. Keep in mind that we are not talking about a few dozen animals, but up to the staggering figure of 250,000!

**Gadhimai Festival**

Now I have never been to, or witnessed this Hindu festival, of Gadhimai, and I would not particularly wish to, however there is the Hindu festival of Dussehra which takes place in the month of October, each year, which is in the Hindu calendar, the month of Aswiyuja. Dussehra is to celebrate good over evil, celebrating when Lord Rama killed the demon-king.

Now I been most fortunate in having witnessed, and taken part in this festival, which can last up to ten days, only because I was lucky enough, as a National Serviceman, to be attached to this famous Gurkha regiment, the Sirmoor Rifles, or to give it the full title, 2/2$^{nd}$ King Edward V11`s own Gurkha Rifles.

Very few people will have witnessed this festival first hand, and compared to the previously described Festival of Gadhimai, this was a "walk in the park"! Armed with my old camera that went almost everywhere with me, I was able to record the whole event.

For me and all of my fellow Gurkhas, plus the officers and their wives, this was the event on the Gurkha calendar which is, perhaps, of the greatest importance. Much work and preparation had gone into the event. Outside seating had been erected for officers and their wives, a sort of stage had been constructed, and a totem pole had been highly decorated, and sunk in the ground. Many live goats had been brought in, plus two bullocks to be sacrificed. Rifles and various weaponry had been neatly set out and displayed, and covered with beautiful wild flowers, with petals from large flowers, adorning them. The Hindu priest in his white robes would sprinkle holy water over the weaponry and at the same time chant a few words. This was all explained to me, that by carrying out this ritual, it would bring good luck to the regiment, and all those serving within it. There was Indian music playing, a great abundance of food, both raw and cooked, with the usual chapatis, poppadoms beer and soft drinks.

Everything quietened down, as the first bullock was led into the area, and its head tied with ropes, held by several Ghurkhas pulling the head to press against the totem pole. Other Ghurkhas had ropes around the animal's neck, pulling backwards, so that the neck was at full stretch. The RSM (regimental sergeant major) then appeared, carrying a large ceremonial Kukri. He was a solidly built man, and stood directly in line, with the animal's neck. With all eyes upon the RSM, he held the kukri, high above his head for a few seconds, to compose himself, and then with a powerful downward blow with the kukri, you could hear the thud of the blade hitting the flesh, and it continued right through with this one foul swipe. There was a great cheer from the crowd as the warm blood gushed from the animal, and the body stood for a few seconds, before it slumped to the ground, and the head dropped, as the ropes were released. A gruesome experience, but one that I perhaps cherish with a greater understanding of their religion, if that is the way to describe the experience.

The RSM then proceeded to the table where Lt. Co. Cruickshank was seated. The colonel stood to greet the man, and congratulate him on decapitating the animal with one single blow, and wound around the RMSs head a white turban, in recognition of a task well done, and one that would bring good luck to the regiment.

The music then started up once again, whilst in the background Ghurkha cooks, and other personnel, including some women were busy slaughtering around two dozen goats. The method was always the same, with one person holding the horns, the other pulling at the back legs, whilst the third used his kukri, to chop straight through the animal's neck. The speed with which they carried out these decapitations was amazing and little wonder that enemies of the Ghurkha was always fearful!

There was a further bullock brought in for the ritual decapitation, and pulled by ropes, into the same position as the first animal. This one was more difficult, as it obviously could smell the blood of the first animal, and was actually standing in the bloodied ground, with a look of terror in its eyes. A Ghurkha cook came forth, and sadly his first blow was not successful, and a second blow was delivered, before the head and body departed, and slumped to the ground. With the gruesome parts of the celebration over, the laughing, drinking and eating carried on. There were a few turns on stage, a Ghurkha comedian, and others telling stories, generally bringing forth laughter, but with music playing and the speed of speech, I couldn't understand much of the proceedings, with my somewhat limited Ghurkha.

**Blessing of arms at commencement of Dussehera Festival**

**Dussehera Festival**

For myself, I was quite lucky to have the chance of a second leave, and this time, I decided to go to Panang Island, which is known as the Pearl of the Orient, because of its great beauty, and it certainly lived up well to its reputation. "Sandycroft" was the name of the leave centre, run mainly by WVS (Women's Voluntary Service). The golden beaches are wonderful to behold, such as Tanjung Bungah, Batu Ferringhi and Telukbahang. Swaying palm trees everywhere, including along the beach areas. The Betal Nut palm is there as well, and produces that nut which the Tamil rubber tappers love to show, all day long, whilst they work. It produces red colour saliva, and that is a bit off putting, when they spit from time to time!

Penang looks out onto the famous Straits of Malacca, a strip of busy waterway in excess of 500 miles in length, connecting India to China by the joining at one end of the Indian Ocean, to the South China Seas at the other end. Piracy has always been a problem with the Straits from the earliest of times that anyone can remember, and still continues today. The capital of the island is Georgetown and I use the word "Island" as in the period when I was there, no bridge connection had been made, and the only way was by ferry. Penang has the oldest Anglican Church in south East Asia. St. Georges.

**W.V.S living Quarters Sandycroft Leave Centre, Penang Island**

Penang was originally part of the Sultanate of Kedah, until it became a British possession in 1796. The island's defence system was the famous Fort Cornwallis. In 1948 Penang became a state of the Federation of Malaya. One of the most interesting places on the island was the Snake Temple, at Sungai Kluang, Bayan Lepas. It was built around 1875 and the temple honoured a resident, Chor Soo Kong a Buddist monk, who had amazing healing powers. I, however, felt the whole place very creepy, with these large and small snakes appearing all over the place wherever you looked. Curled up in branches, or hanging from trees within the Temple.

On the mainland, opposite Penang Island, was a very important military base, known as RAF Butterworth. The main body there was the Australian Air Force, and a certain Valetta aircraft, lovingly known as the "Pig". They dropped leaflets across wide areas of the jungle, giving the bandits a chance to surrender

Dakotas were also used for similar tasks. Also these planes were used for supplying troops on the ground, with food and supplies, as did the Lincoln bombers. Butterworth served as a front line airfield for other units on a rotation basis, such as RAF Changi, R.A.F Kuala Lumpur, RAF Kuantan, RAF Seletar, and RAF Tenagh. It must be remembered that the Royal Navy, the Australian Navy, and the New Zealand Navy also played their important part in the war against the guerrillas.

There were two aircraft carriers deployed, along with twelve destroyers, and four minesweeping patrol ships. The navy was also able to bombard a jungle area of know guerrilla concentration, before troops moved in to a particular area. The little Auster aircraft were also used as lookout planes, sweeping low over the jungle, trying to locate and spot enemy camps, and pinpoint a spot, where a helicopter could deliver by ropes a number of troops, quickly and efficiently. It was very effective in that one moment there were no troops on the ground, and the next moment there were men there, on the ground, fully armed and ready for action. It must be said however, that this could only happen safely where there were sufficient gaps in the dense undergrowth, or a particular area had already been cleared and prepared by ground troops.

It is quite surprising to me that the problem in Malaya, was always referred to as the Malayan Emergency, and never classified as a war. When you look at the statistical figures it would appear to me as ... a "war".

Maybe however, it would be correct to classify it as a small war, as the total number of casualties on both sides was not in the realms of great wars or battles. The number of men and women at arms were quite substantial:

40,000 regular Commonwealth troops
37,000 Special constables
24,000 Federation police
250,000 Malayan Home Guard
Casualties recorded, were 1,346 Malays killed
519 British killed
2,406 Malay and British/Commonwealth troops wounded
Civilian casualties, 2,478 killed, plus 810 missing
There were approximately 8,000 MRLA bandits, plus about 150,000 Min Yuen supporters (Remember these were sympathisers, aiding the bandits with food, supplies etc.)
6,710 wounded
1.287 captured
2,702 surrendered (amnesty was given)

An amazing array of countries, and regiments taking part, such as Australia, New Zealand, Rhodesia, Fiji, the famous King's African Rifles, and others from the British SAS, who took a very prominent role in the many actions that took place.

At the start of the Malayan Emergency, British troops and particularly the British National Servicemen, had not been trained in jungle warfare, as so many of them had only done their basic tainting back in the UK. Tough though the infantry training had been back in the UK, it had not taught them the essential needs and discipline of jungle warfare. They did not know how to live off the jungle foods which were readily available deep in the heart of the jungle, if needs be. How to deal with the many animals that roamed, and the insects which they would certainly encounter, and snakes such as pythons, scorpions and leeches, which could not just be pulled off your skin, as the head would-be rooted into the skin and would cause blood disorders; so a jungle warfare school was set up in Kota Tinggi, and experts were brought in to teach the troops how to deal with anything the jungle may ever throw at them. This tuition brought forth important results quite quickly. The jungle can be a daunting and hostile environment, with its dense undergrowth, and tall trees, blotting out natural daylight, but once you begin to understand the vegetation, and the habits of animals, then it is less intimidating.

To be able to detect the difference of the chatter and calls of real monkeys, or parrots, against similar noises made by the enemy to fool you, then you feel much more relaxed, but must always be alert at all times. Many men from many regiments were able to gain valuable experience from the jungle school, including the Devonshire's, Suffolk's, Somerset, West Yorkshire, Cameronian, Argyle and Sutherland, Gordon's, Gloucester's and many more. Some of the 42nd and 45th Marine Commandos Brigade had also learned extra skills.

Now, up until now, I have not mentioned daily life, with the Gurkhas, particularly in "B" Company. We always rose early, around 6.30am as that was a good time to be up, and about, with the cool air of the night, meeting up with the morning sunshine and a mist rising up from the jungle and surrounding areas. Sometimes calm and quiet, and sometimes with the shrill squeak, and chatter of monkeys, depending where you were.

The smell of curry wafting across the camp; the Gurkha cooks were up much earlier than anyone, preparing the first meal of the day. There would be a vast galvanised bath tub, similar to what homes back in the UK used for the daily bath, particularly the country homes, where modern plumbing had not yet been installed. The rice was steaming hot, fantastically white in colour, and not all caked together as a lump, but the grains of rice still individual. Another great tub of similar proportions would contain steaming hot vegetables, a mixture of various green leaves, and sometimes root vegetables as well ... all curried to perfection, plus a large bowl of dal.

All of this cooking took place outside in the open, and the only off-putting part of the whole thing, was that the Gurkha cooks had a habit of clearing their throats and spitting, from time to time, and one always hoped and prayed that their aim would always be sufficient to miss the large cooking pots, and tubs. It was a known fact that although the Gurkha was an extremely fit person by any standard at all, some of them did seem to have this catarrhal problem.

The other very important item on the menu was the hot mug of very sweet tea (cha). Now that was something to get used to. The cooks would put onto your tin plate as much food as you wanted, and then a ladle of dhal (or dal), which was usually Chana Dal, the yellow Indian chickpea, or sometimes, the Matar dal, the green split pea. Then with my plate of food in one hand and my mug of tea in the other, I would find a spot to crouch down with my fellow Gurkhas, and eat my curry in the same way as they did, with my bare hands.

They consider cutlery to be dirty, and likewise when they smoke a cigarette, it never touches their lips, but they smoke through their fingers, which they had also taught me to do. I always remembered those wise words from Lt. Co. Cruikshank, when I was inducted into the regiment ... "Learn their language ... eat their food ... and respect their religion."

I feel sure that they appreciated that I, as an English soldier, had made the effort to integrate with them, and their way of life, and their habits, and I always felt a sort of "brotherhood" with them. The initial teaching me to swear in Gurkhali, was a typical devilment of soldiers of any nation, but at least they told me what it actually meant.

Now that first meal of the day, which may be referred to as breakfast, would always be curried vegetables. At mid-day there was no food at all, just a large mug of the hot sweet tea, or two mugs of it, if you could drink that much. The second meal of the day was in the evening, when live goats are brought in and slaughtered by the cooks. One man holds the horns, and pulls the animal towards him, another holds the back legs, and pulls towards him. The third man then decapitates the animal, with his kukri, in one swift blow. The animal is then strung up; its stomach split open, and entrails discharged. A blow lamp takes off most of the hair, and then it is chopped up into about one inch spares, and thrown into a cooking pot, and curried; a wonderful amount of rice, and the usual dhal.

Again the cooks will put on your tin plate, a good helping, plus your mug of hot sweet tea, and away you go to your friends, and to eat your meal, again, usually squatting. Now there is sometimes a slight downside to the meal, and that is when you get a lump of goat's meat in your mouth, that still has much of the tough black hair of the goat on it, as the blow lamp failed to get it. This is almost like eating, and cleaning your teeth at the same time!

Now Gurkhas have a caste system, which means that some can eat pork, goat, or lamb. Others cannot eat eggs, and it will be very much dependant on their caste Whilst the highest regarded caste is the Rana caste (perhaps regal), I have never witnessed any difference, or superiority shown by a Gurkha, and I feel sure that the British Army would not permit it.

Depending on the camp you are in, there would often be the sound of Indian music being played, accompanied by the melodious sounds of a male or female vocalist ... and, yes ... you do get used to it, and what was totally foreign to you when you first joined them, becomes quite normal music to your ears. Not exactly "Top of the Pops" ... but makes you wonder, if you are now becoming a real Gurkha!

What many people would not know is that the Gurkhas are given a regular rum ration by the army, which they would drink on an evening, when they were not on duty, or expected to be on duty. It was a general gathering, outside, squatting on the ground, with laughing, and joking, and drinking rum. Several times they tried to get me drunk, but that only happened once ... on the first occasion, and I can assure you that it is far from funny. Just think about the whole thing. It is early evening, and you have just eaten far too much curried goat and rice, and are feeling somewhat bloated, and as you crouch out in the open, with your fellow Gurkhas, drink rather generous amounts of rum, with laughter all around, and you are beginning to fail to understand the language, and the night air is becoming rather oppressive, and you are not sure if you want to be sick or go to the toilet ... or maybe you need both ... Once bitten, twice shy is the motto! Never again. That does not mean, never to partake in the rum ration, but means to take it very carefully, as it can be a long evening!

As for bedtime, in almost all cases, we slept on a charpoy. For those that have never slept on one, or never heard of it, I will explain. It is very common in Asia. It is a bed made entirely of a wooden frame, with four legs, and twine is threaded from side to side and from end to end. A thin mattress is placed on top, and then a mosquito net, over the whole thing. Although we were issued with Paludrine tablets, it was still prudent to have your mosquito net. Mosquito bites were not very pleasant anyway. One would lie in bed at night watching the small lizards run across the ceiling, or roof, as the case may be. They would usually keep perfectly still, and then a mosquito landed within striking distance, their tongue would flash out and consume it. We were therefore always happy to have the lizards around the basha (hut). The one thing we were not so keen on was the Bootlace snake, a thin black or dark brown snake. Very thin, hence the name "bootlace," commonly called the "Blind snake," about 15cms long. Whilst this snake was not poisonous or dangerous like many of the snake variety in Malaya, such as several species of Viper, Krait, and Cobra, he was not that welcome in your bedroom. It was always wise to check any item of clothing which had been left on the floor, in addition to checking your boots.

The majority of Gurkhas were Hindu, with a very minor number perhaps of the Christian faith. The Hindus do like to offer a prayer to their god before retiring. To pray to their Hindu god, a number of them will have a small container hanging from the wall above their bed, containing joss sticks, which give off a pleasant, pungent aroma. And with that there was often a small effigy of Krishna, their Nepalese god, which is the eighth incarnation of Lord Visha in Hinduism. They would offer a small prayer before retiring to bed, and even I found this reverence very calming to see, such brave fighting men so calm and humble before their god.

Now whilst speaking and thinking of brave men, one must immediately think of the Iban trackers. These men were an enormous asset to the British and Commonwealth troops. I met up with some of them on two particular occasions; tough, slightly darkened men, with long hair, often hanging down over their shoulders, and coming from Borneo.

They were usually tattooed all over their bodies, but each tattoo had its own meaning, not just for decoration. For young Ibans, the first tattoo was often the "Bunga Terung." A depiction of the flower of a local aubergine species, and was tattooed underneath the outside edge of the collar bone. These men from Borneo, were tribal, and came from the dense forests of north Borneo and Sarawak. They had incredible skills of tracking. Just by looking at the ground, the undergrowth, they could very accurately confirm what had passed along a track, how long ago, how many people, and what weights they were carrying. One can just realise how valuable these men were when leading a patrol through dense jungle. They were extremely vulnerable, being up front of a patrol, and were the first target of the bandits lying in wait.

These trackers were first engaged on 8th August 1948, a total of 49 of them to commence with, to assist, and track down the communist insurgents; later on, more that 170 of them were engaged. Their leaders back home requested that their warriors be given full military responsibility, and so they were formed into the Sarawak Rangers, a fully-fledged military unit, with Lt. Co. C.J. Bird as their first commanding officer, on the 1st of January, 1953.

There was a particular occasion which I remember well, as it ended up quite amusingly, but at the time could have had serious consequences.

We had to take food and supplies up to a camp on the edge of the Cameron Highlands. Now the Cameron Highlands were named after William Cameron, a British surveyor, commissioned by the ten colonial governments, to map out the area in 1885, a most extensive hill station, the size of Singapore, and occupying an area of approximately 275 square miles, in the Titiwangsa Mountains. The area is drained by eight rivers, the main ones being Bertram, Telom, and Lemol, and the Highlands stand about 5,000 feet high.

The air is cool, as compared with the area below, and has many European style houses, some with a Tudor style, and one can feel very much as if you are back in the UK.

This particular day, the convoy would consist of two Humber Scout cars, one armoured 3 ton Bedford Lorry, and two other covered Bedford 3 ton lorries. The officer in charge was a young newly appointed officer, possibly not that long out of university, and he thought that he knew everything, and was determined to show everyone that he was in charge. Although I remember his name well, I will not mention it, as his type are often the worst type that can be encountered in the British Army. The very best officers are usually, those that have come up through the ranks.

I had done this trip before and knew that the road from Tapah to the Highlands was around forty miles of treacherous road, twisting and turning every few yards. I was driving the lead Scout car, and my gunner, with mounted Bren gun, was Gangebahardur. The rear scout car gunner was this newly appointed British officer, with negligible experience of convoys. I knew, as did the other Ghurkha troops in the convoy that on both sides of the twisting road, were large rock formations, and roughly halfway up the route were always a large number of Rock Apes. This is what we had been told they were. A species of Malay ape often referred to as Batutut. Full height, they would stand around three to four feet tall, but in my opinion they were more like Borneo Orang-utans, and what they loved to do, and were pretty accurate at it, was to hurl lumps of rock, at vehicles at every opportunity.

**Rock Ape**

Knowing the dangers, as we slowly approached the difficult bends, and area where they were most likely to be, my gunner lowered himself into the vehicle, and closed down the hatch, and within seconds, the radio crackled, and the officer in the rear Scout car, was demanding that our hatch be opened, and our gunner return to his position, but the command had hardly been completed, when we heard the sound of rock hitting his Scout car, and his sudden cries!

We were bombarded, but were safe inside, and had to laugh at the situation, which we were almost certain would happen. On arrival at destination, very little was said by the young officer, apart from the fact that he admitted he had been surprised at the ferocity, and force of the bombarding animals.

**The "Ubbly-Bubbly" Man, The Barber with Gurkhas**

Back at camp, life went on as usual, with vehicles to be checked, and maintained to a standard, whereby whenever needed, they would be available. We had two Chinese civilian mechanics, Lee Joc Peng and Lee Ling, both quite knowledgeable, and good mechanics. Apart from myself, there was Jock Thompson. We also had a motor transport officer, who appeared from time to time, a captain Taylor. He was a pleasant officer, obviously based elsewhere and possibly from HQ in Ipoh. When he appeared, he usually asked a few questions as to whether we needed anything, and checked to make sure everything was running smoothly with the vehicles, or if we had any particular problems with any vehicle, where it might have to be sent to large base REME workshops, for something which was beyond our capabilities Our main vehicles were a Bren gun carrier, which could pull a 17 pounder gun, armoured Ford 3 ton lorries, 15 cwt American Dodge trucks jeeps, Bedford trucks, Humber Scout cars, and now and again, a Humber staff car, plus the very heavy armour-plated 3 ton lorries.

It also appeared that captain Taylor needed to kill a bit of his time every now and then, and on more than one occasion he requested that I drive a Scout car, with him as gunner, and we would go off to some destination, sometimes quite a distance away from camp, to another military camp, not always one of our battalion's companies, but to some other regiment. I never did know if he was on a genuine business trip; or if it was to kill a few hours of his day. I did not mind, as I always got along fine with him and he always treated me in a satisfactory and favourable way.

**Humber Scout Car, me adjusting search light**

Back at our camp, we did have the Charwalla, a happy Indian guy, who could offer you his brew of hot, sweet tea, at any time of the day, or evening, seven days a week, at a reasonable cost. Then there was the "Ubbly-Bubbly" man, the barber; again an Indian who seemed to smoke on and off all day, with the bubbling sound of the water, as he drew on it from time to time. Then there was the tailor. An Indian with an antiquated treadle sewing machine, on which he could produce any garment you needed "Sharkskin" was a shirt material of the day, and he could make you a wonderful shirt for around $5. He would measure you at mid-day, and by the evening you could go and collect it ... not that there was anywhere to go!

From time to time I had to report to REME headquarters in Ipoh, and I suppose that it was to make sure that you had a bit of discipline, which you did not get when out with "B" company, where you were your own boss, and ran your day in the way you wanted, with nobody to dictate what you were to do

Meeting up with fellow soldiers was perhaps the good thing about HQ. There was a large NAAFI there, and lots of facilities which you would expect with so many different camps, different areas, and different regiments, and after having a few drinks in the evening, and returning to your particular area in the dark, when you heard the command ... Who goes there? ... You stopped immediately, frozen to the ground, and promptly replied ... Friend!

The Gurkha guards seemed to surprise you most of all, as with their dark faces, and their great ability to appear from nowhere, when you lease expected to be challenged.

There was a great number of lads which I met up with at HQ, such as "Lofty" Oldfield, Roy Holman, Ken Lucan, an ambulance driver, Ron, Jake, Nash, Attain, Fred Cross, Lance corporal Mockridge (catering) and "Bushy" and another called "Bones." Many of these lads I would see from time to time, but most of the time lads were called by their nicknames, so you never knew the person's real name. My Gurkha friends possibly did have nicknames, but I only knew them by what I considered to be their real names, such as Gangebahardur, Dhanbahardur, Eric Williams (yes a Gurkha) Dharamsing, Yambahardur, Ratanbahardur, and so many others.

**L/CPL Mockriage "Cheeta" and Another "Jock"**

It is interesting to note that the Brigade of Gurkhas operated continuously throughout the Malayan Emergency. In 1948 four Gurkha regiments became for the first time, an integral part of the British Army, forming the Brigade of Gurkhas.

2nd King Edward's Own Gurkha Rifles (The Sirmoor Rifles)

6th Gurkha Rifles (Later Queen Elizabeth's Own)

7th Gurkha Rifles (Later Duke of Edinburgh's Own)

10th Gurkha Rifles (Later Princess Mary's Own)

At the time of the partitioning of India, originally there were ten Gurkha regiments, in the Indian army, each consisting of a number of battalions.

Negotiations between the Nepalese, British and Indian governments resulted in four regiments being transferred to the British Army.

Now the Sirmoor Rifles were first raised in 1815, as the Sirmoor Battalion They were the first Gurkha unit in the service of the East India Company. They fought in the 3$^{rd}$ Mahratta War of 1817.

In 1876 they acquired a royal patron the Prince of Wales ... OWN.

In the First World war they served in Flanders. In 1915 they moved to Egypt, and then returned to India in 1916. In the Second World War, they fought in many different theatres. Now as to their headwear, this consisted of the famous Gurkha felt hat, which is their hallmark throughout the world, and different to any other military headwear. It was made by a famous English hat company based in Atherstone, Warwickshire, by the name of Denham, and Hargreave Ltd., who regretfully closed down, several years ago. Made from two felt hoods, blocked together, and then sewn around the edge of the brim, to secure it, as one hat. A leather chin strap, in shiny "patent" finish, and with an inner headband (or sweat pad, as known in the hatting industry). Two eyelets either side and then trimmed with a pleated matching coloured trim, and the crossed kukri motive, sewn over the trimming band, on the left hand side.

The Ghurkha always had a hat, which was at least one size too small for a proper head fit, and often up to two sizes too small, so that the hat was worn, tilted slightly to the right side of the head. This hat was worn with the normal clothing of shirt, trousers, or shorts, long socks, and military boots.

**4 Gurkhas of 2/2<sup>nd</sup> Outside of "Basha. Hats Tilted to Right**

Then there was the ceremonial "pill box" hat. This was small, and round, not to actually fit the head, but to be worn on the head. Colour black, and with a row of black and red check ribbon around the lower edge of the hat. This was the $2^{nd}$ /2nds colours. Usually a black "Pom pom" on the top centre of the pill box, but I have also witnessed a red pom pom ... never really knew why. The "pill box" hat always had a shiny chin strap. Now these pill box hats were worn by members of the pipe and drum band, who I also recall, wore trews, in a tartan, that I could have sworn, was Black Watch. However I checked with the Scottish Tartan Authority, who are based in Crieff, Perthshire, and they informed me that two Gurkha regiments did wear the Black Watch, but not the $2^{nd}/2^{nd}$ Gurkhas!

However, I distinctly remember those trews, thinking how smart these Ghurkhas looked, and how well they played the bagpipes"

Now when it comes to bagpipes, Gurkhas, will give you that wry smile or grin, and tell you quite sincerely, that the bagpipe was invented by the Nepalese shepherds, who tended flocks of goats in the lower hills of the Himalayas, long before the Scots had even thought of such a thing, and long before the Scottish shepherds had thought of hitting a stone with a stick, to relieve the boredom of shepherding, which was said to be the origination of the game of golf! Maybe this is something which will never be proven!

Perhaps when speaking of the cow as sacred, this should be regarded as "taboo." That would perhaps be the better word to use. The Nepalese - as the Indian Hindu - relies very much on the cow for every day survival, when you consider that the cow gives milk, which in turn can be made into ghee, the rancid butter used in many dishes, including curries. The cow is sometimes used for tilling the fields, cow dung for fertiliser. The gift of a cow is applauded as truly the best kind of gift that can be given.

Now new kampongs were constructed, containing sometimes 1,000 people or more. Inside, these villages, or Kampongs, as the Malays called them, traditional houses were built in the "Longhouse" style. Sometimes the largest kampongs could hold up to 5,000 people, in comparative safety. To get a large animal in, or out of the kampong would be impossible without passing the guards at the gate, and likewise with bicycles, and other larger objects. At night the internal areas of the kampong were often lit by searchlights operated from a watchtower by Malay police.

Getting out to go to work on a rubber plantation, or elsewhere, both male and female workers could be searched, and were only permitted to carry enough food out to supply their own needs for that particular day. Checks were made by police and military at check points, and they could be anywhere, on any road, and at any time, and not just to check cars and lorries, but also people with bicycles and even walking. This was very successful in depriving the terrorists of food, which in the past they had forced and coerced the local population into doing, and even demanding sanctuary. Such police, and military checkpoints made the carrying of anything, for the terrorists almost impossible.

One problem still did remain, and that was the problem of the pregnant woman! Sympathisers would place a small or maybe even large bag of rice, up into their clothing, and hopefully exit the kampong and go to work. They would then place the bag of rice by a certain tree, and that night it would be collected by the bandits. We, the military, could obviously not do a search on such a woman, but Malay female police officers could, and so they would stand with male police officers and if required search a "pregnant" woman.

There always did remain Malaya, Indians, Chinese, and Indonesians, that had sympathy for these bandits, who even had in certain areas of the jungle, workshops hospitals of a kind, and their agents, and it was up to the people like us, to make life extremely difficult for them. There were certain "black areas" such as Negri. Sembilan, Johore, Panang, Perak, with most communist activity.

When I took a Gurkha patrol out, they would go deep into the juggle for a few days or longer, I would take them in an open vehicle, so that they were visible, to all, and go a mile or two down the road. I would stop, and the men would then lie down in the vehicle, so that they could not be seen. I would then drive back, past the entrance to our camp, and proceed for a mile or two. The men would then dismount, and disappear into the ulu (jungle).You just had to play the bandits and informers at their own game!

The reason for this method was that by word of mouth, and with lightning speed, the bandits would be informed that a patrol had been taken in such and such direction ... but they hadn't, and it was hoped that by this turnabout a group of bandits might be caught off guard, near to where I had dropped the patrol.

In an earlier paragraph I mentioned, Sir Gerald Templar, the most senior British officer that any British soldier might ever meet. He had a most illustrious career in the British Army, and to give him his full title, he was Field Marshall, Sir Gerald Walter Templar, KG GCB GCMG KBE DSO. He was a British military commander that had fought in two world wars. He succeeded Sir Henry Lovell Goldsworthy Gurney, who was the High Commissioner in Malaya, on 22$^{nd}$ January, 1952.

Things dramatically improved, with Templar's decision to win the hearts and minds of the people, rather than just put more troops on the ground.

**Sir Gerald Templar Departing From Tapah After His Inspection. October 1952**

In October, 1952, I, along with fellow Ghurkhas, was in Tapah on a routine operation. Sir Gerald paid regular visits to many different units of troops throughout Malaya, to give encouragement, and thanks for their efforts. This was typical of a man that had come up through the ranks over many years, and was therefore highly respected by both officers and troops, police and all of those engaged in the conflict.

I had at that moment in my army career, the pleasure of meeting him on his fleeting visit. His helicopter landed on the local football ground, adjacent to where we were at the time. He spoke to several of the officers and men gathered there, and had a few brief words with me, asking how long I had been in Malaya, and if I was enjoying my time with the Ghurkhas. After a comparatively short period, he was back in the helicopter, which was parked on the football pitch, and then up, and away. Although I was lucky enough to photograph the arrival and departure of his helicopter, it was far more than I dare do, to photograph him, although he possibly would not have objected, but it was just not the thing to do at that particular moment. No one knows if this was just a chance visit, or whether it had been arranged in advance, by the powers that be!

People must sometimes wonder what soldiers do in their leisure time, when not on duty. Well, I can only speak for the Ghurkhas in "B" company. Some would read, some listen to music, some would chat, but many would still keep fit, by playing volley ball, a game which most of them enjoyed, and were good at. Despite their height, it is quite amazing the heights to which they can jump, in order to get the ball over the net, and take a point and the power with which they would hit the ball was quite extraordinary, as I found out on many occasions when playing with them. Whilst I was perhaps taller than many of them, and I was in a forward position to hammer the ball over the net, up would come one of their opposition players, jumping as high as the net to put a clock on the ball which I was hoping would give us a scoring point, and advantage.

Football was another game which they enjoyed, and we had an area of grass, both long and short and tufted, which was somewhat awful terrain on which to even contemplate a serious game. However, most games were not too serious, and were played in bare feet. Now at the beginning, I found this extremely difficult, especially if you keep in mind that footballs were made of leather in those days. I felt quite proud that I, as an Englishman, could emulate them in that game.

On one occasion we were stationed in a town called Raub, or to put it correctly, just on the outskirts of Raub.

Within the confines of our camp area, there were some large trees, and looking up into the higher branches we could see two very large cats making hissing noises, maybe at one another, or maybe just for the sake of making a noise. They did look somewhat intimidating, even from the height they were. I had never seen such large cats, and they were possibly three to four times the size of a domestic cat. Speaking to a local Malay, he said that they were perhaps a "flatheaded cat and the other a clouded leopard cat. The markings you would get on a domestic "tabby" cat, but the animal was far too large for that. The Malay informed us that they could be dangerous. My fellow Ghurkha and myself decided that it may be perhaps much safer to destroy them, rather than having them wandering around our camp, but how could we bring them down. A normal rifle, using .303, would be out of the question, as it was far too powerful, and where would the bullet end up? A much smaller type of bullet was required, and so we decided upon a .22 rifle. That decision was possibly a mistake, as these two cats were stronger than we had anticipated.

We each put a bullet into each one of the animals, but they still stood there, on the branches, so we quickly fired a second bullet into each one of them, and they both remained upright for a short period, just a few seconds, and then they both dropped to the ground with thuds. They certainly were large by comparison to domestic cats. They were something that I had never seen before, and were certainly connected to the very much larger cats of the jungle.

Speaking of cats of the jungle, there is the Malayan Tiger, a fearful animal to look at, so I was told, but also elusive and fearful of man. During my time in Malaya, I had spoken to many different infantry troops that went into the jungle on patrols, on a regular basis, but none had ever come across a Malayan Tiger.

The lads permanently based in Ipoh did have a pet monkey on the camp, and it had become a very popular creature, and would be passed around from person to person, and particularly if you had something which he liked to eat.

Another animal that I learned had been found in camp was a wild boar, and there were many of them in the jungle, and very dangerous creatures they were.

This particular one, I could not make out, as a creature such as this would normally not stay around long, but would revert back to the jungle as quickly as he could possibly escape. It was said that if you could get his attention, make him angry, he would chase you, with head down, and at full speed. Again it was said that by standing just by a vehicle's wheel, and remaining there, until the very last second, then side stepping, the boar would charge right into the wheel at full tilt! A strange game to play, and perhaps a bit cruel ... but it may not even have been true!

Now many roads in Malaya were very good, straight roads, but there were also more that were twisting and turning, with heavy undergrowth on either side. Much had been cut down by local authorities to keep the sides and edges of jungle visible, and not so easy for the bandits to attack passing vehicles, but there was always the chance of problems happening in the most unlikely of places. Sharp bends on downward sloping hilly roads were always a danger, and a favourite ploy of the guerrillas was to place a large broken tree trunk onto the road, or better still, across the road. A military vehicle being driven at a fair pace and rounding a corner, could run into such an object, and have its front wheel or wheels, plus axel, damaged and brought to a halt, and beyond repair. The REME would inevitably remove such vehicles, and, depending upon the severity of the damage, would either take them to the company or regiment, from whence they had come, or get them put into a large REME workshop that could deal with anything, no matter how badly damaged.

That is why most military vehicles on remote roads were nearly always accompanied by armoured scout cars, or a larger fully armoured vehicle. Various objects would be placed on the road, at tricky and difficult points, which could not be detected until the very last moment, and a vehicle would have to swerve to avoid such objects, resulting in perhaps a skid on a slippery surface, and going over an embankment, or into a ditch.

This did not always mean that there would be bandits waiting in the undergrowth to fire upon the stricken vehicle, but in many instances that was the case, and the whole idea of the operation, and that is why it was unwise for a vehicle to be on its own, without an escort.

**R.E.M.E Team Recovering an Army Vehicle**

In order to mount certain of these operations, the bandits would have lookouts on higher ground that could quickly pass information along from one to the other, notifying the ones that would lay the trap, exactly what military vehicle was on its way.

Now as one can imagine, to recover a vehicle was sometimes a very tricky operation for the REME, depending on how, or where the damaged vehicle had ended up, and could take just a few minutes, or sometimes hours, and if in a remote area the recovery team would need cover, just in case the bandits took advantage of the situation.

REME would have extra armed men, or they would possibly have armed Malay police to guard whilst the recovery operation was in progress.

Despatch riders were seldom seen, or sent out by the military, as that was a death trap for any rider. Just a thin wire across the road, from one tree to another, at the correct height, and that could mean total decapitation.

The army had a basic, and common sense rule to deal with ambushes, and that was that if going up a steep incline and receiving a crossfire ambush, or even an ambush from one side of the road the convoy would have to halt, and return the fire, but if on the other hand, the vehicles were coming down hill, it would usually be more prudent to accelerate, and drive through the ambush.

I was part of a smallish convoy, with a scout car as the lead vehicle, then three lorries, me being in the third vehicle of the three and a scout car behind me. Strangely, it was the road that we all knew so well, taking us up to the Cameron Highlands. I suppose that everyone gets a bit complacent about such things, when you have done it several times, and without incident, and despite all the warnings and discipline which you are taught, to be alert at all times, sometimes there is a lapse in your concentration. This early morning trip was just one of those days. As we climbed higher and higher, and thinking perhaps more about the apes rather than human beings, when we suddenly heard the sound of automatic fire, and the "ping" of bullets as they hit the rocks at the side of us.

Fire was immediately returned by the gunner on the lead scout car, and Gurkhas in the lorries quickly returned fire, as our convoy came to a jolting stop. Several men leaped out of the back of their lorries, hiding behind the rear wheels to get cover, which in turn directed the enemy fire, towards the rear of the lorry in front of me. The scout car behind me was pouring out an enormous amount of lead, and within a minute or two the ambush was all over and done with, so I stood guard with another Gurkha over the vehicles, whilst our fellow soldiers checked the undergrowth, both sides of the road, in the high rocks to see if we had managed to kill or wound anyone.

No luck, the bandits had disappeared without trace back into the ulu. We reckon that they had been laying in wait for some time, and were well positioned above us, and perhaps should have done better, but then, they may have been surprised that our convoy was a Gurkha one and did not fancy getting tangled up with men that used kukris as their favourite weapon! They should have been more vigilant, and noticed the 2/2$^{nd}$ Gurkha insignia on our vehicles.

The day ended fine, we delivered what we had to, and returned to camp, and it was not until we were back there, that someone pointed out that I had a small tear in my canvas jungle boot, and a tiny spot of blood. It was not until I removed my boots that I felt a twinge of soreness and discomfort. I have the tiniest piece of shrapnel that had gone in, just under my big left toe.

I was admitted to the military hospital, where I was able to see the fantastic dedication of the Queen Alexandra's nurses. Apart from the guy who was in the next bed, and had been circumcised, which brought much laughter from several of the lads, as the nurses brought him bromide from time to time to placate his arduous feelings, possibly brought on by them anyway!

Two Gurkhas were brought in, and placed in beds opposite me. They appeared like pieces of raw meat, and the reason for this was that they had been carrying phosphorous bombs, possibly on their waist belts, when they had exploded. One Ghurkha was raw from the waist downwards and the other from the waist upwards. One would have said that they had no chance of survival, and each was placed on the beds, and a curved bamboo frame put over their bodies, and a white sheet placed over the frame. This avoided the sheet touching their skin.

**Recovering at the Change of Air Station, Cameron
Highlands. After Coming Out of Hospital**

Doctors attended them, and it appeared that they were
removing some of the skin, as apparently, phosphorous sticks
to skin, and eats into it. It cannot be wiped off, and removal of
skin is possibly the best way to go. Every hour or so, the frame
and sheet were removed, and the old under sheet, covered in
blood removed, and a new sheet put down. Two nurses sat
with them, day and night, and after just a week, I left hospital,
but was later told that these two Gurkhas had survived, and
recovered almost completely ... thanks to the army doctors, and
the dedication of the nurses.

I was sent to a recuperation centre for a few days ... up in
the Cameron Highlands, believe it or not!

When speaking of a patrol, this generally means a group of infantry men going into the jungle for a few days, but sometimes there were those patrols which were referred to as "deep penetration" jungle patrols, and they could go into the jungle for weeks at a time.

The normal jungle patrols would consist of nine men or more, or perhaps fourteen men, and sometimes included an Iban tracker, but usually a patrol would be without that assistance. Depending on the operational need, and the period of time that would be spent in the jungle, things were decided upon that basis.

The standard jungle outfit was - starting from the head - a face net, which was seldom used, as it could impair vision. A floppy jungle hat, a shirt, tucked into the trousers, and the trousers tucked into the canvas and rubber boots. A poncho was also carried, and was a must against the torrential rain, particularly in the monsoon season. All of his clothing was in jungle green colour. The ponchos could be stretched out over saplings or available branches, at night to protect those trying to get a few hours rest. It was usual to take it in turns to do a two hour "stag", which was a guard duty, keeping very alert, with possibly a Bren gun. Nights in the jungle can be very daunting, with the sound of creatures creeping or scurrying through the undergrowth, the occasional chatter of a monkey, the squawk of a parrot, or even the simple thing of a rotting branch crashing to the ground. Sometimes straining your eyes, thinking that you are seeing something which is really not there; even for those trying to rest on a groundsheet, the ants do not cease to move, and cause discomfort. Now on top of all this discomfort, there were medical problems which would add to your troubles, such as scorpion stings, prickly heat, ringworm, ulcerated sores, scrub typhus, tinea, snake bites, plus the leeches, and the foot rot.

A patrol did carry single bladed razorblades, so that a snake bite could be dealt with, by making a tiny cut, where the snake had bitten and the poison squeezed out, matches that would ignite, even if wet, and these were for the leeches, and the best way to remove them. Keeping in mind that so many of these soldiers were National Servicemen, and had really been thrown in to this type of warfare. Little training or knowledge of the Malayan territory, particularly the jungle which had so many creepy, crawling insects Fast flowing rivers to cross, stinking swamps, with millions of mosquitoes, biting red ants, and the denseness of the Attap palms, the bamboo, and the creepers, all of these things sapping your strength. A tough challenge for the infantry.

Speaking to one another whilst on patrol was very unwise and instructions and directions were mainly by hand signals. Obviously to light a fire was out of the question, and so rations were mainly "dry pack". With the excessive body heat from climbing and descending, fresh drinking water was usually at a premium, but adequate supplies were carried but always used sparingly. At certain times fresh, clear water could be obtained from a stream, which was always a bonus.

**Dead Bandit Being Tied to Bamboo Pole**

Now in the early days of the emergency, when the Gurkhas made a kill, they would decapitate the bandit, and carry the head, or heads, back to the camp, to prove to their officers that they had killed! Unfortunately, a communist paper in the UK called the Daily Worker, had a front page picture of a Gurkha holding the heads, with a caption stating that ... "This is what British troops are doing to the enemy," or some such similar statement. It was therefore decided at that moment, that every patrol should be issued with a camera, to record a kill. Many of the top bandits were well known, and so photographic evidence was extremely useful to the military.

A general instruction was made to all regiments that if one could take a prisoner, do so. What to do with him or her would always be a problem however, particularly when you are deep in the jungle, as he or she, would become the greatest liability and danger to that patrol. Perhaps, fortunately, very few prisoners were taken due to the fact, that for both sides, it was shoot to kill, and that usually was the end result.

On the other hand when a guerrilla had been shot, and brought down, it was extremely dangerous to approach him as there had been instances of a soldier approaching what was thought to be a very badly injured bandit, or a dead one, and at the very last moment he would let off a hand grenade, killing the British or Commonwealth soldier. Chances like that could not be taken.

If the patrol was two or three days or more from the pickup point on a road, where the patrol would be collected, the body should be photographed and buried, as a patrol usually carried a small lightweight spade. If on the other hand, the patrol was only a day's trek from a main road, then the body would be tied to a bamboo pole, and carried back. It would then sometimes be displayed outside a police station for a couple of days, with a notice above it, stating that this is what happens to would be bandits, or words to that effect!

What sort of weaponry did a patrol carry? That very much depended on the regiment, and the thoughts of what may be required to deal with every eventually. The leading scout, which was the most dangerous position in the patrol, would possibly carry a Browning 126 auto 12 bore shotgun, with the barrel sawn off. The reason for such a weapon is because the jungle being so thick, visibility is often ten feet or less. This means that upon seeing a face or part of the enemy's body, you have one chance only, otherwise you are dead. The twelve bore effects such a volume of shot, that some of it will certainly hit the enemy ... and hopefully in the face, and having fired, the leading scout would drop to the ground, allowing the number two, to fire with his Sten gun, or maybe 9mm Owen MK1 sub machine gun, and finish the enemy off. Then there was the M1 Carbine, the Lee Enfield, M2 Carbine, and the DeLisle machine gun which Sir Gerald Templar had tried out, and found it an ideal weapon. There was plenty of choice for the patrols, but the man at the rear of the patrol may have carried a lightweight Bren gun, as he would be sometimes moving backwards from time to time, guarding the patrol from the rear. A most important part of being in a patrol was to make sure that you never lost the sight of the man in front of you; otherwise you would be in dire trouble. Keep taking the Paludrine tablet, which is proguanil hydrochloride, an anti-malarial ingredient!!

At the end of the patrol, it would be back onto a road, at a given point, on which a vehicle would pick up everyone. Back at camp and exhausted, one could look forward to removing all the sweaty, stinking clothing that had been with you for many days. A shave to get rid of that beard or stubble which you had grown, and then under a shower to give your body that much earned special treat. Then the next stop would be to the doctors, to get him to check you over. Most of the time, whether you had foot rot, tinea, ringworm, or just prickly heat, the doctor would paint you with gentian violet liquid, and more often or not a green liquid, and a yellow liquid, so your body would end up looking like some Picasso painting. In fairness to the doctors, whatever they painted on seemed to work within a few days, and you were back to normal.

From time to time, Gurkhas, like any regiment, do from time to time, and perhaps more so in "war zones" love to have entertainment, taking their minds away from the day to day tasks which they have to perform. These fighting men often have to produce their own entertainment, where professional entertainers are unavailable.

On one particular instance, it had been decided that some entertainment would be created by these Gurkhas on a certain date, at a certain time, and there was the usual buzz about who would be the performers, and what they would do, and what was about to take place, would be the usual singing, perhaps dancing, and comedian routines, which could in fact be very funny.

I was invited to take part in a sketch, and after much discussion, it was decided that my part would be that of a wounded soldier, needing hospital treatment. Only because we were all young men, supple and fit, was it possible that I could carry out my particular part. The idea was that I should be dressed completely in the standard jungle green outfit, complete with the canvas boots. However, my left leg was to be bent backwards, and tied up, to hold it in that position. A young palm tree was to be cut down, and the softest green trunk the thickness of my leg was to be cut into a length exactly equal to the distance from foot to knee joint. It was coloured to a pinkish, white, and then placed into my left canvas boot. The inside of the palm was gouged out at a certain spot, and a fine skin, maybe a goat or pig bladder, filled with blood, and tied, was inserted into the hole in the "leg." This artificial leg was then secured to my body by means of string or something. This was the plan. I would need to be assisted up onto the small stage that was to be constructed, simply because the artificial leg would have no real movement, other than to swing back and forth.

On the evening of the entertainment, the many rows of seats were filled, and that included not only the men, but also the Gurkha officers, and a couple of British officers, which had come to support the event When it came to my turn, there was already on stage a large table and also a Gurkha doctor/surgeon, dressed with a white apron. As I walked in, supported by my two fellow soldiers, also dressed in jungle green outfits, there was much chatter, and laughter from the audience.

There was then great conversation between the "surgeon" and my two supporting soldiers, obviously asking what had happened to me. I had been badly wounded in the left leg. The talking, plus the laughter was not possible for me to totally understand, but it was pretty obvious that this "surgeon" was going to sort out my problem!

I was then helped onto the table, and the "surgeon" spoke a few words, with more laughter from the audience, and the "surgeon" produced a kukri, rolled up my left trouser leg, and with one almighty swipe he chopped off my leg, making sure his knife went through at the exact spot where he concealed bladder had been placed. Blood shot out all over the "surgeons" white apron, much to the approval of the audience, with cheers and clapping. Our performance had been a great success!

This does pose the question. Does the Gurkha have a traditional and inbuilt desire for the kukri and blood? I do not think so, as today the Gurkha is a modern soldier of the British Army, but maybe in the past, long, long, ago, his warrior forefathers may have had a different outlook.

As I have mentioned previously, it would be wrong to pick out any particular regiment for extra special praise, but there is one corps, which I consider as, unsung heroes ... the Cinderella of the Malaysian Emergency, and that is the RASC "Royal Army Service Corps). These are the lads that deliver the goods to the troops. The majority of these drivers were National Servicemen, who travelled all over Malaya, to towns and villages, or wherever supplies were needed, driving along dangerous roads, hilly roads, and roads which at any time could be ambushed, and hardly ever did these lads have escort cover.

Almost every item of kit, replacements of anything, and most of all food, they were the ones delivering. Now the food supplies could have been a tricky problem, but the military, who were always capable of solving most problems, had been able to work out a system of supplying the food packs, which were particularly required for those patrols entering the jungle, for days or weeks at a time. Some were Muslims, some Buddhists, Hindus, Christians, but the common food acceptable to all, was rice, so the basis of the pack, was rice. Then vegetables Meat could be killed in the appropriate way, acceptable to the particular religion, then curried and cooked in a traditional manner, so that every religion was able to have what they would normally eat. Distribution by the RASC had to be precise, and the right packs, with the right content, to the right regiment!

Some lives were lost, it is sad to say, but considering the thousands of miles that they travelled, and the thousands of tons that they carried in their vehicles, they have a very proud record of service during the twelve years of the emergency.

I think that because I was not an officer, but just a craftsman in the REME, and attached to the Gurkhas, I was able to associate with them fully, in a way that an officer was unable to. The majority of men that I was with, were mainly Hindu, as I have already mentioned, and there was one or two who were Christian, and no doubt there were some who would have been Buddhist, but I cannot remember coming across them, but then on the other hand, the question of religion was not discussed in any real depth, apart from the times when I spoke to them about the things which were correct to adhere to, and honour, and the thing which would, or could show disrespect to their religion.

Did I ever make any mistakes, during my close association with them? Yes I did, purely from total ignorance. One day a few of us were out on a sort of "walk-about" not an official patrol, and were not that far from camp, but we were armed. We came upon a small, cool, very inviting lake, and a few of us decided to take a dip, whilst the others stood guard. The

Ghurkhas did remove their clothing, but left their underpants on. I stripped off completely, and at the time, it did not really dawn on me, as to why they had retained their underpants. Back at camp, I was informed, by a good Ghurkha friend of mine that a Hindu man, must never see another Hindu man totally naked ... bad mistake, but something to remember!

Now the Gurkha was paid less than me, and that is the way it was. A British soldier, doing exactly the same job as a Gurkha, would get more pay, and that always seemed to me, and many others, terribly unfair. On top of my pay, I got a small amount extra, which was for a food allowance. I was supposed to buy European or British type foods, either fresh, or tinned, whenever I had the opportunity, but I never did, as I enjoyed so much my full integration with these men, and their wonderful curries. Whilst I have already explained the morning curry was always vegetables, the evening one was meat, and generally goat's meat, but every now and again, some men would shoot the odd wild boar that had strayed too near to the camp, and that made a nice change of diet. Another thing which we all had every week, was a free tin of Players cigarettes, always issued to those on active service. For those that did not smoke, they could always sell them, as there were always plenty of buyers in those days.

**Gurkhas With A Wild Boar Which They Shot**

Now these Gurkhas got leave, to go home, and during this period there was a leave, known as a Long Leave, where they could be away for almost six months, I believe. That was later stopped. I think that most of them used to return home, via Darjeeling, but exactly by what route I do not know. What I do know however, is that the journey home, could take many days. Arriving on Nepalese soil, some would hire a mule to do a part of the journey, and then they would relinquish it at a certain dropping off point, and continue their journey on foot, climbing higher and higher, up through the mountains, and their passes, for maybe three or four days. For Europeans, living mainly in low lying area, we find this quite incredible, but then if you look at the map of Nepal, and look at the different districts, area, and villages, you can see the problems they faced. To live in places such as Mumgaon, Charpur, Syang, Bagarchhap, so remote, or even the lower places, such as Bidur, or Jakarkat, you can appreciate the task ahead of them.

Even today with much better facilities for the ex-gurkha soldier, the pensioner, he still may have to walk for a whole day or more to collect his monthly pension, from a welfare centre in Pokhara, This town was always a centre for boys applying to become a Ghurkha, serving within the British Army; a recruiting centre. Many of them would never have managed to see or visit their capital city, Kathmandu. Keeping in mind that Nepal had always been controlled by a monarch, but in 1951 the monarch ended that particular system of rule, and a cabinet system and government was installed, which was something of an entirely new innovation, and never tested before.

Friends of mine have often over the years, asked me many questions, relating to my time in Malaya, and to my period with the Gurkhas, and it has not always been that easy to respond with the right answer, because I simply did not know.

One question that has come up from time to time is the one regarding the kukri. The knife I have already explained is never thrown, the notch near the handle is to stop blood dripping onto the handle, and making it wet, but what about the other two small knives in the scabbard? One is called Karda, and that is a general utility knife. The other, which has a blunt edge, for sharpening the kukri, is known as a chakmak. I also understand that most Gurkhas back home in Nepal, would have a second kukri, which is used for every day work or chopping or cutting. The "best" kukri, to use such a word, is the one that every enemy has come to respect ... a razor sharp knife, used to kill!

Now, finally, the question put to me was, did I ever get into trouble whilst serving my National Service? Regretfully, the answer is yes ... once.

I had been out on some mission, and it had been an all-day event. Cannot remember where, or what we had done, but I do remember getting back to camp, and feeling quite tired, and decided not to "pull through" (clean) the barrel of my rifle that evening, but to put it in the armoury, and take it out early next morning, and clean it.

I was up the following morning, nice and early, went to the armoury, and requested my rifle, and much to my surprise, it was not here. It had either been removed that previous evening or very early this very morning. I immediately realised what the consequences would be ... a charge!

I was duly charged with having a dirty rifle, and was marched in to Lt. Colonel Cruikshank, minus my beret, which is the norm. He demanded to know what my excuse was, and I explained the situation, but to no avail. He gave me, fourteen days loss of pay, and I was quickly marched out again.

The REME played a most important part during the Malayan Emergency. Apart from the specialists in armoury, the likes of myself, trained in mechanics, not only dealt with the mundane jobs of maintaining vehicles belonging to our regiments, there were large workshops dotted around Malaya, where very major repairs could be carried out on the largest of vehicles Damaged body work, armour plating damage, and many major jobs beyond the capabilities of the local REME mechanics within various companies attached to various regiments. Hundreds, maybe thousands of vehicles were used on a daily basis, taking troops out to drop off the patrols. Armoured scout cars, doing escort work. Large armoured Ford or Bedford lorries, used for carrying troops, anywhere, at any time. Vehicles collecting foods and ammunition ... the number of uses were endless.

It was quite obvious with so many vehicles in operational use on a daily basis, that there would be accidents. The very nature of many roads in Malaya, with steep hills, twists and turns, falling trees or rocks. Roads saturated, during the monsoon season, and the torrential rain, plus the damage caused by the communist guerrillas, either by way of gunfire, when a vehicle was ambushed, or by the logs, and other objects which they had placed at certain spots in the road to endeavour to de-stabilise the steering of the vehicle, as so to cause a serious crash.

**Myself Loading Vehicles For Larger R.E.M.E Workshops
in Singapore**

It was the REME that was responsible for the recovery of such vehicles and we were well equipped to deal with these situations. Whilst we did not have the practical experience of such recovery back home, during our course at Norton Manor, much of this sort of work was very much common, and needed logical thinking to appraise a situation when confronted with it, and almost every one was different Where to place the ropes or chains on a large overturned vehicle, how to lift a vehicle that had a broken front axle, and many recovery jobs that just needed a modicum of thought before embarking upon the actual task.

The sturdy Scammell recovery vehicle was a godsend to us, in that this monster of a military vehicle was so powerful, that it's pulling ability, its winch gear, would deal with anything we were confronted with. It had a six speed, constant gearbox, plus reverse, and the model was known as the "Pioneer." It could cope with an armoured Ford or Bedford, which had come off the road, and into a waterlogged area, with reasonable ease, considering the enormous weight it was being asked to pull. I therefore have many photos of various vehicles in problems, which often looked unsolvable, but in fact were routine to the REME with the various recovery vehicles on which we could rely.

It was fast getting towards the end of my time in Malay, and for me it was perhaps a sad time, as I had met, and been friends with so many of the Gurkhas. A couple of days before I was due to leave I had a wonderful surprise when they presented me with another kukri, in a scabbard, complete with the sharpening knife, and the skinning/general purpose knife. This now meant that I had two kukri knives, and that was good news, because the British Customs law at that time was, that if you had one knife, it was classed as a weapon, but two knives were classed as an ornament, where you could hang them on a wall, crossed, which represented, an ornament! I did have the two of them chromed, and they looked superb.

Before leaving, it was suggested to me that I might consider joining the Malayan police force, as many ex-soldiers had already done that, I was also approached by the army, suggesting that if I signed on for a given number of years, I would be promoted. However, neither of these offers particularly appealed to me, and I thought that perhaps after all, it would be nice to return to the UK.

The day that I left for Singapore, on my way home, I had a raging tooth ache, and my face was slightly swollen one side. On arrival in Singapore, I visited a military dentist, who took one look at me, and declared that I would not be permitted to board the ship, like that He took a good look at my teeth, and said that I had an abscess, and that he should not really extract the tooth that was causing the problem, until the abscess and swelling had gone down, but under the special circumstances of my immediate repatriation he would, with my permission, remove the tooth! Great relief and the swelling went down fast much to my joy.

I was now able to join the troopship, the Empire Windrush, and we sailed from Singapore on the 3$^{rd}$ of February, 1953. Now the Empire Windrush had quite a history. Once again, built in Germany, but later taken as a "Prize," by the British. Back in 1948, on the 22$^{nd}$ of June to be exact, she had arrived in Tilbury with 492 passengers from Jamaica, who had wanted to settle in England.

Just one year, after our departure from Singapore, whilst in the Mediterranean, March 1954, and situated just off the coast of Algeria, the ship had a serious explosion in the engine room, which killed four crew. Fire broke out and spread quickly, but over 1,200 men, women and children escaped unharmed, and were rescued, ending up in Algiers, when the ship sank. It had in fact had trouble whilst in transit along the Suez Canal, with engine problems.

**Empire Windrush**

The Empire Windrush was painted in the troopship colours of that period, white, with a blue line running along the length of her sides, high up towards the upper deck. The ship had not started her journey from Singapore, but in fact had come from Korea, carrying various military that had served in the Korean War, including a number which had been wounded. The hospital on board was of a reasonable size, and both day and night, there were guards on duty, inside and outside of the hospital, for security reasons. I had to perform a guard duty, and was posted inside the hospital on two occasions, and was most surprised to see some of the injured were suffering from dental problems, which in today's terms, would be classified as post traumatic stress, caused by the experience of war. They were in cots, with high sides, to prevent them getting out of bed, in exactly the same way, as you would treat a baby. I suddenly recognised one of these patients, and it was the same soldier that I had travelled out with on the Empress of Australia, in 1951. He was the same guy that had the bright idea of buying the whole sheet of numbers, when playing, "Housey Housey".

I tried many times to remind him of who I was, how we had been together on the journey out to Singapore, but he had no recollections at all, and was completely void of any conversation.

I did ask one of the medical orderlies, if they knew anything about his history, and how he had been affected in the way he was, but they had only understood from information given to them, that he was in a Land Rover in Korea, when it hit a land mine. He was blown up in the vehicle, and his state of mind was all due to that experience. I was also informed that there was an important military hospital in Southampton for various types of battle injuries, and that is the place he would possibly be sent for treatment. Having seen the condition of several of the soldiers, in that hospital, it brought it very clearly to my mind, how lucky I had been, during my time in Malaya.

Maybe not quite so lucky on the Empire Windrush, as somewhere during the passage across the Indian Ocean, there was a problem with the ships steering gear, and we spent a whole day, going around in a circle. This maybe was a much lesser problem than that of the Empress of Australia, on our journey out, when the main propeller dropped off!

**The author with Gurkhas**

For many National Servicemen, their time in the military had been a pleasant experience, either in the UK, or perhaps somewhere around the world, at many destinations where they were required. For others the whole experience had been a nightmare, and for those on active service some had ended in total tragedy, and were buried far away from their homeland. Men, resting there in Korea or Malaya forever, and those other Men, returning home, at just twenty, twenty-one and twenty two year's age. The vast majority knew and understood that it was a duty to do for the nation at that time.

Like many wars of our time, it is difficult to assess if they were ever worth the time, the effort and loss of life. In the case of Malaya, there appears to be a reasonable amount of stability in the country, and it has become a popular destination for tourism. As for Korea, there is still the great divide, between north and south, with a constant nervous tension, which persists, due to the actions of the North Korean regime.

Back home with my parents once again, and settling into the routine of civvy street, I had a notification that I would have to do three years T.A. (Territorial Army) service. The notification also mentioned that I was to be attached to the County of London Yeomanry (Sharpshooters), based at St. John's Wood, in London. It would mean a few evening attendances and parades each month, plus a fortnight away each year, for the three years. Quite exciting stuff ... tanks!

Hardly ever seen one, never been in one, but now was my chance. Salisbury Plain, and Castlemartin Tank Range in South Wales, those were the venues, during the three years. The tank range at Castlemartin was my first real experience of tanks, and that was mainly as an onlooker, because the tank drivers and gunners had previous experience, and were lined up along the coastal edge, and were firing at an object, being towed by a small ship a short distance out at sea. To be quite frank, I really felt that the gunners were not particularly that good, as their "misses," outnumbered their "hits" by a substantial number.

Nearest town of Tenby was OK, but a bit quiet on a Sunday. Most people at Chapel and no pubs open to get a drink. After a few enquiries however, we did manage to find a local person who was able to show us where the men of Tenby went for a drink. A club, tucked away from all visitors and strangers, but when found ... full of the "Locals" to almost overflowing, and all downing pints, and the air thick with smoke.

Castlemartin tank ranges have a very long and interesting history, which many readers will not know about, other than those that were military personnel, sent there for training

Way back in the 1930s,this land was acquired by the Ministry of Defence(MOD)The land covers about 5,900 acres, and comes within the bounds of the Pembrokeshire Coast National Park. A rugged, rock strewn coastline.

The ranges are used for about three quarters of the year and when being used, has an exclusion zone of about 22 kilometres off the coast. When not being used by the military, the general public can use the area for walks and general recreation. In the period of 1970/80,the Royal Armoured Corps used the range extensively for their famous Chieftain tank, and today at the entrance to Merrion Camp, Castlemartin is displayed another famous tank, the Centurian MK12.

Now I did not know hardly anything about this part of the UK but once again, thanks to my National Service commitment and Territorial army experiences, I was now able to learn so much about this particular corner of the UK...Pembrokeshire, South Wales.

Now during the month of May,1961,the 84th German Panzer Division tanks drove through the streets of Wales, on their way to Castlemartin! There was at that time, as one can imagine, a great deal of controversy, particularly from the older generation, who remembered the bombing of Pembroke Docks, but others who appreciated the fact that the second world war had been over for some time, and that now, the Germans were part of the whole strategic defence force of Europe.

Fortunately, the anti German feelings did not last too long, and the German soldiers made every effort to adhere to local customs, and way of life and to integrate and assist the local population in many ways.

Part of the reason that these Panzers were at Castlemartin was due to the fact that in the north of Germany, there was very little suitable land to train with tanks and furthermore the British Army of the Rhine had the same problem.

In 1995 Castlemartin had commenced to be used also for infantry training and small arms training, often using live ammunition to give more realistic feeling of real battlefield conditions.

It is said that over the period of time that the Germans were at Castlemartin, some 84,000 of them were trained there, and that was up to 1966.During that time the Welsh/German entente-cordiale must have improved dramatically, as around 140 Welsh girls, married German soldiers.

Whilst I was at Castlemartin I did visit Tenby, as I have already said, which was a holiday town in the making, and today has become such and is a very popular holiday destination. Towns back in the 1950s were very dull and uninteresting as compared to the world of today but many of them held a wealth of history, such as Milford Haven and Pembroke Dock, which I visited by taking out an army vehicle on a "road test". Such were the privileges of a REME soldier of the TA, attached to the County of London Yeomanry !

Milford Haven, founded in 1793 by Sir William Hamilton, was used as a port, way back in the Middle Ages. Milford was chosen as a base for some 1000 American troops who were stationed in the town during the second world was, and played a key role in the preparation for "D" day! Although it is the 3$^{rd}$ largest deep sea port in the UK, and the largest in Wales, it managed to avoid serious bombing during the Second World War.

However, Pembroke Dock was not so lucky, as they were bombed and the one extremely serious bombing was when the Luftwaffe had a Junkers JU88, flying up the Haven, delivering its load of bombs upon the oil tanks, sited at Penar. A fire raged there for eighteen days!

Later in 1943, the RAF decided to station its Sunderland flying boats there….lots of them…. therefore, it became the largest concentration of flying boats in the whole world.

Pembroke Dock, Milford Haven, Tenby and Castlemartin. A far cry from Singapore, Kula Lumpur and the Cameron Highlands but just as interesting and educational and VERY much safer.

Now moving on to Salisbury Plain, this was a more exciting venue, and so much open space! We were lined up on a parade ground there and the sergeant in charge, asked who had driven a tank before, and requested that they take two paces forward. Strangely, nobody stepped forward. He asked again, and this time I decided that I world step forward, as I was dying to get inside a tank.

The sergeant requested me to climb into the tank, and at the same time requested another sergeant to climb up into, or onto the turret. Once inside, no steering wheel, but just the two steering levers, either side. Foot pedals much the same as a car or lorry. The sergeant on top was resting his feet very much on my shoulders, and it was he that would indicate where I was to go, left or right. He asked me to start the engine, but I did not have a clue where the starter was, and could not see a starter button anywhere. He asked again, and I had to apologise, and say that I had not driven this model of tank before!

All I remember him shouting out was that the starter button was right behind my head. Yes, it was ... pressed hard, and the thing roared into life. Away we went, steady at first, but once getting the feel of the thing, speeded up to a fair pace. We were now out in open country, on ground that gradually became more rugged, the further we went, and eventually I was instructed to climb up a fairly lengthy hill, not that particularly steep, and getting near the top, I slowed to a crawling pace, as I realised, we were quite high up, and then a sheer drop of maybe twenty feet or maybe twenty five feet.

I was instructed to balance the tank at the top, which I considered I did quite well. I was just looking out at distant space, and the tank was slightly rocking. The instruction was then to advance slowly. I gave the accelerator the very slightest of touches, and the nose of the tank dipped, as we started to go down the incline. Amazingly the tank rolled down the steep incline, tracks turning, but I could also feel the sliding, and as we hit level ground once again, I was able to relax more. Through water hazards, bends and various terrain, and eventually turned back, to where we had started. I was congratulated on my driving and handling ability of this monster, which was either a Comet or Centurion tank. From then on, for both annual camps, which were carried out over Salisbury Plain, I was permitted to drive and went out on several missions, driving a Churchill ARV Armoured Recovery Vehicle). This was a heavy clumsy tank, that had the turret, and most of the centre parts removed, but was ideal for going out to recover tanks that had got themselves into problems, but its petrol consumption was frightening. When towing another tank, you were obtaining bout four gallons to the mile!

I was quite surprised to realise how tanks could get into problems, but were usually caused in my opinion, by drivers that were trying to be too clever, and getting the tank into impossible terrain and situations. The number of times we were called out to a tank, whose driver thought he would drive through water, not knowing how deep it was, and not knowing that the ground below was like a swamp, very muddy and extremely soft. The result was usually that the belly plates of the tank had sunk so low into the water, and the thick mud surrounded its tracks that the more they turned, they were turning on the spot, sending the vehicle deeper and deeper into the ground with mud and water covering its drive wheels. Luckily for all of them, the REME were at hand, because that is what we were for!

Tanks cannot use normal roads, as their tracks would do so much damage to any road surface, and so they were transported by road, on a tank carrier. The vehicle used at that time, was the mighty Diamond T. An American vehicle that usually pulled a trailer, with a great number of wheels, and the tank was driven up, onto such a trailer. Now with the weight of the vehicle, trailer and tank, you could be talking of anything up to about seventy five tons! With such an enormous load, you needed a number of gears, and so this Diamond T had around ten gears, plus a booster, which could give even more. It really was a monster to drive, but once you had the hang of it, and could get it on the move from a standing start, it was quite fun, and I enjoyed the experience.

Finally I must say that the whole of my time doing National Service was a most wonderful experience, and for those lucky enough, or unlucky enough, not to have experienced it, they really did miss an awful lot. Granted the first few weeks of getting "broken in" is perhaps not the most pleasant of experiences, but once you become a real soldier, it is most rewarding, particularly if you are fortunate enough to be sent abroad. What you see, and what you learn, the experience, and friends you make is worth so much in your early life, and particularly in the period of which I am speaking, long before holidays and travel abroad was heard of.

It does appear that the majority of those that experienced National Service have grown up to be good citizens of the UK ... not all of them, but the majority, and many arguments have arisen over the years as to whether it was a good thing or not. It did teach you to be respectful to others, to work together as a team, and to understand, and respect peoples of other nations, their religions and their habits.

I hope that my experiences here in this book, along with the accompanying photographs, will bring greater understanding of the Malayan Emergency, of the Ghurkha soldier, and what National Service was all about. My thanks to the British Army for such a wonderful time!

Independence came to Malaya in August 1957, under Prime Minister Tunku Abdul Rahman.

The last resistance from the MRLA guerrillas ended with their surrender at Telok Anson, marsh area, in 1958. Many of the remaining pockets of guerrillas fled to the Thai border, and Chin Peng their leader, received political asylum in Beijing, China, where he spent the remainder of his life.

As for the Gurkha, during the period of the 1950s he was really getting a rough deal, in the opinion of many. After his service with the British Army, he would be released, and would return back home to his mountain village, without any real money, and his retirement years would be in virtual poverty, with a total lack of medical facilities, and in many cases, no running water. He still had his wife to support, and had to endeavour to scratch a living from his small plot of land, with a few chickens, maybe a pig or goat, which gave him milk and cheese. The luckier ones may have even had a cow, which was so valuable to them, for their butter, cheese, and also to make ghee, for their cooking.

Fortunately, and eventually, in the years that followed, things did improve slightly, and the Gurkhas' terms of engagement improved in wages, and help from the British Army. In addition to that, the Gurkha Welfare Trust, based in Salisbury, in today's world, looks after those ex Gurkhas, and their spouses that remain in Nepal. Monthly pensions do have to be collected from the pay centre, in Pokhara however, and that does mean that for some of the old soldiers, they do have to track from their hillside abode, for a whole day, to reach the payment centre. Medical attention is at hand with fully trained doctors and nurses, and two care homes have been built in Pokhara where the elderly and those not able to look after themselves, can come to be residents, and see out their remaining years. All of this is afforded by the donations of ordinary members of the public in the UK. People that wish to honour the debt owed to these brave men. There is also a Ghurkha Museum, in Winchester, which is well worth a visit, and where souvenirs can be purchased, the proceeds of which go to help the Gurkha fund. In more recent years, ex Gurkhas that have chosen to live in the UK, have found a niche in the labour market, and many of them are now engaged by various companies as security personnel, as they are fit, totally trustworthy, and could deal with most security problems that arise. P & O have engaged quite a number of these ex Gurkhas on their cruise ships.